It is my honor and g
man of God who has touched millions of people globally. Mike
French was one of the pioneers to take the gospel to the Soviet
Union after the fall of communism, reaching thousands in
great crusades and establishing a multitude of churches.

Mike is one of the last great evangelists of our generation—
and a man who believes that every man was created to believe.

As a friend who has observed his ministry these forty years
I can say he is not only a world-class communicator with keen
insight to the human soul, but he is also a man of honesty and
integrity, a man I believe in and can follow.

Mike has a passion for all people but especially hurting
people, whether in Russia or the American ghetto.

One of my greatest memories was watching him reach out to
two thousand disenfranchised people at the Los Angeles Dream
Center. On that night he spoke with such passion and love that
he stayed five straight weeks as a great revival broke out.

Created to Believe is one of those books that could change
your life, a book you'll want to pass on to those you love.

—Tommy Barnett
Author; Co-Pastor,
Dream City Church, Phoenix, Scottsdale, Glendale;
Cofounder, The Los Angeles Dream Center

Mikel French's first book *Created to Believe* is an expertly
crafted devotional that I truly believe will capture the heart,
mind, and spirit of readers. Mikel has been a personal friend
of mine for over twenty years, and it has been a true honor to
watch his ministry and his faith grow over the years. *Created to
Believe* is a book about thinking bigger for Jesus, and it includes
simple and practical advice to do just that. In just ten minutes a
day this book will transform the mind and heart of readers and
usher them into a new mind-set where big thoughts and big
dreams are the norm. I am so proud of Mikel for writing this
first-rate devotional, and I strongly endorse it, as I know it will
change the life of every reader.

—Matthew Barnett
Pastor and Cofounder,
The Los Angeles Dream Center

When I think of people who have impacted the nations of our world, Mikel French comes to my mind. His passion, love, and heart to help people achieve God's best for their life has been a motivating fuel to my personal life.

I have had the privilege of seeing firsthand how God has used Mikel to inspire crowds of multiplied thousands of people to discover and pursue their God-sized dream. In the nation of Russia alone, Mikel has assisted in the funding and planting of hundreds of churches. I shudder to think about what Russia would look like today without the influence of Mikel French's ministry.

If God has ignited a dream in your heart—or perhaps you have yet to discover God's dream for your life— *Created to Believe* is a must read.

—LUKE BARNETT
SENIOR PASTOR, DREAM CITY CHURCH, PHOENIX, AZ

Perhaps the most important thing to say about the material in this devotional is that it has been proven and tested under the fires of adversity during incredible challenges over the past twenty–plus years.

Mikel French was one of the original pioneers who joined OneHope when we were given the opportunity to distribute the first legal Scriptures in the Soviet Union after seventy–plus years of atheism. There were no Christians available to do the distribution that the Soviet government had asked us to do, so we had to seek out dedicated people, who sacrificed to travel and live under almost unendurable conditions. Mikel was one of the very first to join that group of distinguished pioneers. Others came, got some pictures, and never returned. Mikel has continued to minister to the people of Russia for now more than twenty years and more than one hundred trips.

These messages have been fine-tuned in the fire of the front line. They will encourage and challenge you to expand your faith, believe for more, and have confidence that God will give victory.

Thank you, Mikel, for your faithfulness, and thank you for this powerful message.

—BOB HOSKINS
FOUNDER, ONEHOPE

Mikel French is a personal friend, and he is an enthusiast for Jesus. His love for the Lord has taken him around the world to share the good news of God's love. I've ministered with him in Russia, where he has faithfully evangelized over the years, and seen firsthand the fruit of his ministry and the love of Russian believers for him. He is a man of faith, and that's why *Created to Believe* is such a powerful daily devotional. He lives what he writes. The devotionals come from both his believing heart and mind. Your own faith will be lifted as you walk with Mikel through this thirty-day devotional journey.

—Dr. George O. Wood

General Superintendent,

General Council of the Assemblies of God

I have practiced having devotions for decades. It is an important part of my day and my spiritual walk with the Lord Jesus Christ. I have found the devotional *Created to Believe* to be a blessing to me. The devotional thoughts and applicable illustrations from a colleague, brother in the Lord, and my friend, Mikel, will be another stepping stone in the journey with the Lord. I pray you are blessed, encouraged, and challenged to think like Jesus.

—Greg Mundis

Executive Director,

Assemblies of God World Missions

Mikel French is a godly man and a great friend. He knows how the world works and the difference Christianity can make. *Created to Believe* has the combination required to help us understand and apply our faith daily.

—Ron Woods

Pastor, The Assembly, Broken Arrow, OK

CREATED TO BELIEVE

MIKEL FRENCH
WITH STEPHEN KUERT

CREATION
HOUSE

Cover design by Chad Smith

Visit the author's website: http://mikelfrench.org

Library of Congress Control Number: 2017940074
International Standard Book Number: 978-1-62999-221-1
E-book International Standard Book Number:
978-1-62999-222-8

While the author has made every effort to provide accurate telephone numbers and Internet addresses at the time of publication, neither the publisher nor the author assumes any responsibility for errors or for changes that occur after publication.

The author and publisher have attempted to find every source quoted in this book. Any information found after this printing will be included during the first reprint.

18 19 20 21 22 — 9 8 7 6 5 4 3

Printed in Canada

CONTENTS

Preface: Opening the Heart xi

Acknowledgments...xiii

Introduction: The Power of Thoughts xv

Prologue: Speaking to the Heart...xix

PART 1

Think Big: *The Mind of Christ and Regeneration*

Day 1   The Heart 1

Day 2   God's Promise for the New Heart 5

Day 3   The Transformation of the Heart................................... 9

Day 4   The Power of Faith...13

Day 5   To Believe or Not to Believe... 17

Day 6   Belief and the Foundation of Covenant...................... 23

Day 7   Belief and the Experience of Glory................................27

Day 8   Belief and Surrender..31

Day 9   Belief and Direction 35

Day 10   Belief and a Word-Filled Heart 39

Day 11   Belief and an Overflowing Heart................................... 43

Day 12   Belief and the Action of Faith 47

PART 2

Act Big: *The Mind of Christ and Personal Transformation*

Day 13   Momentum: The Action of Faith 54

Day 14   The Seed of the Woman: Transformation
          for Our Feet 58

Day 15   The Seed of Abraham: Transformation
          of Our Hands... 63

Day 16   The Seed of David: Transformation
         for Our Heart 67

Day 17   Transformation in Vertical Relationship 71

Day 18   Transformation in Horizontal Relationships 75

Day 19   Transformation in Internal Relationship 79

Day 20   Transformation in Thinking 83

Day 21   Transformation of Love 86

Day 22   The Challenge of Transformation 90

PART 3

Go Big: *The Mind of Christ for Holy Action*

Day 23   A Call to Holy Action 96

Day 24   The Qualification for Holy Action 99

Day 25   Prayer and Holy Action 103

Day 26   Vision for Holy Action....................................107

Day 27   Risk and Holy Action.......................................111

Day 28   Compassion and Holy Action......................... 115

Day 29   Holy Action and the Miraculous 119

Day 30   Holy Action and the Harvest...........................123

Epilogue...129

Go-Big Answers 131

Notes 135

About the Author..137

Contact the Author..138

OPENING THE HEART

T HE RAIN WAS gently falling that Wednesday October night in 1991. The parking lot was covered with wet leaves as my wife, Marsha; our twelve-year-old son, Jon; and I walked into the elementary school auditorium in Columbus, Ohio. I was to speak there that night. There may have been a hundred people belonging to the young Capital City Church, started by Pastor Jim and Renee Palmer.

Prior to speaking I could feel anticipation as we all witnessed the power of the Holy Spirit opening our hearts to Pastor Jim's words: "God is taking us on an adventure into the heart of God."

His words penetrated my thoughts. I believed that his words were God speaking directly to me. Out of everything he said in his introduction of me, those are the only words that I remember.

To this day, I believe that was the first word that God used to speak to me about my involvement and love for the people of the former Soviet Union and the nation of Russia. God was opening my heart to something that I could not even dream possible, taking me on an adventure into the heart of God.

ACKNOWLEDGMENTS

THE BOOK THAT you are about to read was definitely accomplished by many people. It took a team to help me. My natural gifting is to speak to men and women's hearts, and even though I enjoy writing, it definitely took a team to help me get this accomplished and done.

First of all, thank you to my lovely wife, Marsha, who has been helping me edit thousands of pages for many years and whom I love with all my heart. She has stood by my side and believed with all of her heart that a move of the Holy Spirit can change anything. I love you, Marsha. Thank you for always believing in God, believing in me, and believing in your family.

Second, I want to thank Stephen Kuert. Without his extraordinary abilities there is no way that this book would ever have been finished. He has taken my messages and probed my thoughts to help me find the exact words that were needed to express my heart for this devotional, and all while keeping me focused.

Thanks to Des Evans, who is not only my friend but who also has inspired me with his messages to think deeper thoughts in the Word of God.

Next, thanks are in order for Rebecca, my personal assistant, who has constantly been there and has helped keep everyone, from Creation House to Stephen Kuert and myself, centered.

Last, what began the thoughts of this book was a message in one of my father's books that is over one hundred years old: "The New Heart" by Thomas Guthrie. I would recommend anyone who loves great messages from the past to find it and read it.[1]

INTRODUCTION
THE POWER OF THOUGHTS

Thoughts. Neuroscience teaches us that we have somewhere between fifty thousand to seventy thousand of them a day.[1] Like swarming mosquitoes, thoughts zip in and around our mind. They form the basis of our decisions, inform our actions, and frame our perceptions. Proverbs 23:7 tells us as a man thinks "in his heart, so is he" (KJV). Thoughts control us. They determine our future by forming our present.

Every thought is a seed. The old expression articulates this principle well:

> Sow a thought, and you reap an action; sow an act, and you reap a habit; sow a habit, and you reap a character; sow a character, and you reap a destiny.

The majority of the time, however, these seeds produce a harvest of character weeds and destiny destroyers. We reap the results of bad thinking. Our world is full of such examples: lustful thoughts eventually destroying marriages, selfish thoughts eroding families, and greedy thoughts corrupting entire nations.

For the Christian, this should never be the case. We are called to leave a legacy on this earth. Our lives are destined for kingdom greatness. We have purpose. We have a high calling in Christ Jesus. There is only one way this can become a reality—think His kingdom thoughts. Kingdom thoughts are faith-filled, love-saturated thoughts that summon us to action. This kind of thinking is dangerous to the forces of darkness and the status quo of our generation.

My heart is captivated and challenged by those that step out of the rhythms of routine, the rituals of the usual, and go beyond circumstances, people, places, and things. They dared to risk, they dared to dream, and they dared think big, faith-filled thoughts.

Left to our own sinful nature, our thoughts are doomed to a cycle of perpetual destruction. The selfish thought eventually becomes the unbridled action, producing unholy habits and a corrupted character. The final nail in the coffin is the destiny of death.

What is the solution? Is there no way to turn the cycle around?

With the grace of God, this cycle can be reversed. Kingdom thoughts can produce anointed actions and holy habits. Christlike character and divine destiny can be our portion, provided that we do one thing. We must think like Jesus. In this generation of corruption and perversion, heaven is looking for Jesus-thinkers, those who dare to think the thoughts of the King. These are thoughts of life and liberty to set captives free.

How can I be so sure? The apostle Paul challenges us to have the same mind-set that Jesus possessed (Phil. 2:5). The King James Version makes this abundantly clear: "Let this mind be in you, which was also in Christ Jesus."

We are to think His thoughts. In so doing we adopt His mind-set and His attitude. Let this settle in. We are to think as Jesus thought while on Earth as well as think the thoughts that Christ still thinks in heaven. This is the ultimate idea behind Paul's instruction in Romans for believers to possess a renewed mind (Rom. 12:2). The idea is that we are called to have our mind made new.

Christ's thoughts permeating our mind produces His newness in us. We are no longer abased to servitude by the sinful nature, mere pawns of Satan to serve as captives of the darkness. Rather, His thoughts liberate us. His thoughts transform us. His thoughts motivate us to holy action.

This book is a petition to Christians everywhere to embrace our calling of participating in the mind of Christ. This will enable us to think BIG, like Jesus. This is based on regeneration. We have spent enough time in the past thinking small, doubt-filled thoughts. When we begin to think BIG thoughts we are empowered to take BIG action.

This choice of redirecting your thoughts now can lead you to the place of seeing personal transformation. Finally you will be able to go big in pursuit of holy action!

In the following pages let us examine together the critical role that faith plays in every part of our lives. Believe God for great things!

Go big—believe!

GO-BIG QUESTIONS

1. Every thought is a _____.

2. Our lives are destined for _____.

3. Left to our own sinful nature, our thoughts are doomed to a cycle of _____.

4. With the _____, this cycle can be reversed.

5. What type of thoughts do you have on a daily basis? Share your thoughts below.

_____

_____

_____

SPEAKING TO THE HEART

OUR AMERICAN TEAM boarded the old, faded, orange-and-tan Russian bus in Moscow for what felt like an unending eight-hour drive. We passed through green, lush forests, rolling hillsides, and uneven pastures all the way to the small community of Sevsk, Russia.

The Book of Hope team consisted of pastors from across the United States—many of them, including my father, experiencing Russia for their first time. This was my first opportunity to travel with and work beside Bob and Hazel Hoskins, the leaders of the Book of Hope project and personal heroes of mine.

Our arrival in Sevsk was complicated. There were problems with the local government officials, who were not sure they could trust us, wondering about our real purpose for being there. We were the first Americans to visit the city since the fall of communism, but by a miracle of God's grace the door had opened to go to the first local school.

In that school one of the city officials joined us. As we entered the auditorium, beautiful, young, vibrant faces gathered and soon surrounded us. I was asked to speak first. I asked the audience the three major questions everyone wants to know:

1. Who are we?

2. Where do we come from?

3. Where are we going?

"These questions were all answered in the life of Jesus Christ and can be read about in the Book of Hope. Jesus came to reveal to us who we are, where we have come from, and where we are going," I explained. "He died for our sins because He wanted us to know Him and receive these answers."

I was not allowed to give an invitation to receive Jesus, as one of the city officials had warned us from doing so. When I finished speaking I could sense that there would be some difficult conversations to follow between Bob Hoskins and the city mayor. Later, Bob told me that she was, indeed, very upset with my message. If we did not change it we would not be welcomed to visit any other schools. "Mikel, you've done nothing wrong, but to be honest, I don't know what we should do," Bob admitted.

Some of my dear friends, Pastor Dennis and Sue Lacy, were traveling with us. Once back on the bus, Sue spoke to all of us: "I believe God wants me to speak at the next school." We agreed.

At the school she asked the young students, "How many of your parents raise a garden?" Every child's hand lifted. "I raise a garden also. I am just like your parents," she smiled. "I have a garden so that I can provide my children with the healthiest food so they can grow strong. I think that is why your parents raise a garden; they want what is best for you. How many of you think that your parents want you to have good, healthy food?" Again, every hand went up, and smiles filled the room, including that of the lady mayor.

"The most important gift I have ever given my daughter is found in the Book of Hope. When I read to her about Jesus, she said, 'Mommy, I want to accept Jesus.' I led her in a prayer, and she invited Jesus into her heart. Jesus wants the best for you. Your parents want the best for you, just like your schoolteachers want the best for you. They want you to live a good life. Knowing Jesus is the best thing that could ever happen for you," Sue concluded, and thanked everyone for the opportunity to be there. Everyone in the room clapped.

One of the teachers asked for Sue to teach them the prayer she had taught her daughter, and Sue readily agreed. "Would everyone here like to learn that prayer?" The response was immediate: the entire room wanted to invite Jesus into their hearts and surrender their lives to Him.

When we surrender our heart to Jesus and open our mind to His Word, He heals our broken heart with His forgiving love. He captures our imagination with unlimited possibilities through the power of the Holy Spirit. He fills our thoughts with His awesome promises, which we are created to believe.

> Let this mind be in you which was also in Christ Jesus.
>
> —PHILIPPIANS 2:5, NKJV

PART 1

THINK BIG

THE MIND OF CHRIST AND REGENERATION

DAY 1
THE HEART

OUR HEARTS WERE created with an amazing feature: the ability to believe. We are created to believe. Even more wonderfully, our hearts have been given the ability to believe in God.

Faith directed toward God must always pass through the channel of the heart. It is the heart that must be regenerated by the power of the Spirit. Once we experience the miracle of believing on the Lord Jesus Christ, our heart comes alive for the purposes of God.

The moment that Jesus was invited to change our heart by faith through grace, we were given His righteousness to reign and abide in our lives. This is the good news of the gospel of Christ, as well as the foundation for God's eternal kingdom. The King regenerates our heart and enables us to live in the reality of His kingdom.

Kingdom life enables us to live our life seeing through Christ's eyes. It enables us to demonstrate His heart to every person, in all places, in all situations, and in all areas of our life. One of the primary ways that this lifestyle becomes a reality is by thinking Jesus's thoughts, embracing His attitude, agreeing with His decisions, and implementing His actions in our lives. We are to live in the constant reality of His life, His death, His resurrection, and His overcoming power flowing through every facet of our lives.

God's Word shows us there is a direct correlation between our heart and thoughts. Paul helps us make the connection in the Book of Romans. Many say that reading the Book of John is seeing the gospel through the eyes of the Savior, while reading the Book of Acts is seeing the gospel through the eyes of the Holy Spirit. Reading the Book of Romans gives us a glimpse of the glorious message of redemption through the eyes of God, our Father.

When reading the Book of Romans we see the equivalence of a legal document written from the eternal Judge. It breaks down

1

our walls of guilt, condemnation, fear, and weakness so that you and I can fully grasp the reality of Christ's redemptive work on the cross. Paul's transformative insight in this book draws us into God's power-packed truth. His primary intention is for us to know God's righteousness and to embrace His Son's free gift of His righteousness for ourselves. Righteousness is the idea of right standing before a judge. In other words, it is standing in the right place and being seen as innocent in trial.

In a courtroom, if the accused is innocent, then the lawyer presents the liberating evidence to the judge. The argument goes something like this: "My client is innocent and has never broken the law." The other aspect of the law applies when the client is guilty. In this case, the lawyer seeks out the mercy of the law, finding a way to open up the heart of the judge for grace to be applied to the guilt.

In Romans Paul isn't writing a letter representing us to God. He's writing a letter from the eternal Judge to humanity. The argument is clear: we will be without excuse when we stand before God. Romans 3:23 tells us, "All have sinned and fall short of the glory of God" (NKJV).

Yet, mercy has been extended to the person who believes in Jesus Christ! We stand in the courtroom of judgment, but Jesus is our Defender. We are guilty, but Jesus took our sins and punishment, and He declares us innocent before God the Father, our Judge. By faith in Jesus Christ we are not only saved from sin; we stand justified, without sin, in the eyes of God.

In Romans 10:6–11 Paul articulates the intricate connection of righteousness between the mind and the heart. The heart receives the benefit of salvation from the mind entering into agreement with the truth of Christ's Word.

Let's look at the passage together:

> But the righteousness based on faith says, "Do not say in your heart, 'Who will ascend into heaven?'" (that is, to bring Christ down) "or 'Who will descend into the abyss?'" (that is, to bring Christ up from the dead). But what does it say? "The word is near you,

in your mouth and in your heart" (that is, the word of faith that we proclaim); because, if you confess with your mouth that Jesus is Lord and believe in your heart that God raised him from the dead, you will be saved. For with the heart one believes and is justified, and with the mouth one confesses and is saved. For the Scripture says, "Everyone who believes in him will not be put to shame."

There is an elaborate eternal connection between the mouth and the heart, our confession and faith, and our thoughts and experience of His righteousness. Faith forms from thinking on and believing the truth of Christ's Word. Faith-filled thoughts lead to confession of faith in Christ. This confession coincides with the regeneration and transformation of our heart. Faith in Jesus transforms us; it transforms our heart and renews our mind and releases heaven's righteousness into our life.

Paul's glorious revelation in Romans shook all of Christianity during the reformation of the church, as Luther discovered that righteousness is based on faith. As we experience God's gracious gift in the human heart, the way we think is transformed. His righteousness gives us a believing heart. This concept is critical for seeing God's power work in our lives. We will go into more detail about this later in this book. For now, let's look at how this heavenly transaction of faith and righteousness in the human heart happens.

When you believe and act in faith, you are not the one doing anything. You are simply calling out to God and trusting Him to do it for you. That is how you receive salvation. With your whole being you embrace God setting things right, and then you say it, right out loud: "God has set everything right between Him and I!"

God is able to set things right in our heart because Jesus took our sins when He died on the cross. We receive a new heart—a heart with no hindrances, obstacles, or barriers between God and us. Our heart is free to believe and receive everything that He wants to give us.

Think big—believe!

GO-BIG QUESTIONS

1. The moment that Jesus was invited to change our heart by faith, through grace _____.

2. _____ has been extended to the person who believes in Jesus Christ!

3. God is _____ to set things right in our heart because _____.

4. What are some areas in your life where you could better demonstrate Christ's heart? Share your thoughts below.

_____

_____

_____

GOD'S PROMISE FOR THE NEW HEART

T
HE HEBREWS CONSIDERED the heart to be the very core of one's being and the residence of the soul. *It is where the deepest, innermost part of man resides and where thoughts, will, and motives are generated.* The heart was and still is viewed as the single most important factor in a person's life. The state of a person's heart is reflected in their thoughts.

This is why the ancient writer of Proverbs stressed the importance for us to "watch over your heart with all diligence, For from it flow the springs of life" (Prov. 4:23, NASU). The heart has tremendous importance! Guarding one's heart is the most critical aspect of the new believer's life.

Proverbs sees the condition of the heart controlling the direction of everything in life. It is like a spring that overflows into family, relationships, work, and culture. A pure spring nourishes souls and allows faith to grow and become intuitive. In contrast, a contaminated spring is toxic and causes one's mind to become confused and filled with doubt. So it is essential to keep the condition of the heart pure before God.

When Adam made the tragic mistake of inviting sin into his life in the Garden of Eden he indelibly contaminated the heart-spring of humanity. His sin has passed on to each successive generation. Each generation has had to deal with the curse of sin: sickness, sorrow, death, contaminated relationships with others, a broken relationship with God, and Satanic oppression.

Humanity was in dire need of regeneration. So God made a promise!

The closing chapters of Revelation capture God proclaiming the finality of His messianic purpose: "Behold, I am making all things new" (Rev. 21:5). In this one statement the ultimate purpose of heaven and of the kingdom of God is summarized: Jesus came to make all things new! Everything in life is made new to prepare us for our new home in heaven. Revelation 21:1–3 tells us:

> Then I saw "a new heaven and a new earth," for the
> first heaven and the first earth had passed away, and
> there was no longer any sea. I saw the Holy City, the
> new Jerusalem, coming down out of heaven from
> God, prepared as a bride beautifully dressed for her
> husband. And I heard a loud voice from the throne
> saying, "Look! God's dwelling place is now among
> the people, and he will dwell with them. They will
> be his people, and God himself will be with them
> and be their God. (NIV)

This glorious theme of promise is developed throughout
the Word of God. One of the great Puritan preachers, Thomas
Guthrie, expressed this idea well in his message called *The New
Heart*:

> Jesus is the mediator of a new covenant, the author
> of a new testament, the founder of a new faith. The
> redeemed receive a new name; they sing a new song;
> their home is not to be in the Old, but in the New
> Jerusalem, where they shall dwell on a new earth,
> and walk in glory beneath a new heaven.[1]

What a beautiful picture. *Jesus makes all things new.* The
Cross of Christ reverses the corruption of sin, self, and Satan,
which has caused such death and destruction. How is this
accomplished? The most important aspect of this imagery of
newness relates to the human heart. Only in our heart can true
life be reborn. It is in the heart that God's promise is able to
take root, and it is from the heart that new life can blossom.

The Old Testament prophet Ezekiel declared the foundation
of the new covenant. (See Ezekiel 36.) *God promised to give
humanity the ability to experience a new heart!*

> I'll give you a new heart, put a new spirit in you. I'll
> remove the stone heart from your body and replace
> it with a heart that's God-willed, not self-willed. I'll
> put my Spirit in you and make it possible for you to
> do what I tell you and live by my commands. You'll

once again live in the land I gave your ancestors.
You'll be my people! I'll be your God!

—EZEKIEL 36:24–28, THE MESSAGE

The Lord promised something new in the unfolding plan of redemption through His covenant people. The power of this promise cannot be overstated. For the first time in humanity's history, God promised to deal with the internal nature of a creation set on the path of sin. In order to be saved from our own sinful nature, our heart must be changed. It must be renewed! What a tragedy it would be to miss the beauty of the kingdom of God because we never allowed the Spirit to work the newness of God within our heart.

Without God's work of grace in our life, being able to experience God's new kingdom is totally unattainable. An old, sinful heart can never experience the glories of the new heaven. How tragic to stare at the ultimate promise of the kingdom's beauty and yet be disqualified due to our own sinful nature, which was never transformed by a renewed heart.

God's answer to humanity's dilemma is not external but rather internal. It is the promise of a new heart and a new spirit. Christ changes us and gives us a heart that now delights in doing the will of God. It frees us from the tyranny of selfishness. Our new spirit connects us with His Holy Spirit so that we can know the mind of God! A new heart and new spirit result in new thoughts. We now have the power to be Jesus-thinkers and to engage with heaven's strategies and purposes.

In order to consider the context of the promise, let us look at what God said in His Word. Revelation 21:3–4 sets the stage for heaven's promise:

> And I heard a loud voice from the throne saying, "Behold, the dwelling place of God is with man. He will dwell with them, and they will be his people, and God himself will be with them as their God. He will wipe away every tear from their eyes, and death shall be no more, neither shall there be mourning, nor

crying, nor pain anymore, for the former things have passed away."

Death is no more. Tears are wiped away. Pain is a distant memory. God's ultimate desire for a relationship and ongoing fellowship with His creation is accomplished. We are His people. He is our God! What a breathtaking picture of God's promise, brought forth by the renewing of our heart. A new heart is the passport that allows us into all that has been promised to us.

Only when we put our faith in Jesus are we enabled to experience the glorious reality of the promised new heart. It is here that we can truly connect with the big thoughts of heaven. When we accept Christ we accept adoption into heaven's family, eternal intimacy with the King, destruction of humanity's ultimate enemies (sin and death), and the new order of the kingdom of God!

Think big—believe!

GO-BIG QUESTIONS

1. _____ is where the deepest, innermost part of man resides and where thoughts, will, and motives are _____.

2. Proverbs sees the _____ controlling the direction of everything in life.

3. God promised to give humanity _____.

4. Based on your thoughts, what is the current state of your heart? Share your thoughts below.

_____

_____

_____

THE TRANSFORMATION OF THE HEART

A NEW HEART IS *a transformed heart.* What makes the gospel so impactful is that it has the power to accomplish what nothing else can! It transforms people from the inside out. The power of the salvation message takes people from darkness to light, from satanic bondage to Spirit-empowered living, from being in the kingdom of tyranny to the kingdom of sonship.

How does this invisible miracle happen? This glorious transaction occurs in the heart.

Paul tells us in Romans, "If you confess with your mouth that Jesus is Lord and believe in your heart that God raised him from the dead, you will be saved. For with the heart one believes and is justified, and with the mouth one confesses and is saved" (Rom. 10:9–10).

Confession of the mouth and belief in the heart are not two separate steps to salvation. They must be united together for the heart to transform. The order, however, is less important than their inseparability.

Saving faith requires inward belief and outward confession. These essentials of faith belong together. Salvation comes through acknowledging that Christ is the Lord God and believing in Him. Belief without confession is denial. Confession without belief is ritual. Both belief and confession must occur for Spirit-empowered transformation!

Heart faith is true confidence in the unseen and is based on God's Word. It involves a total commitment of one's self and interests to the demands of Christ's truth. It is similar to the trust children have toward their father and mother. Young children take their word at face value—often with no questions asked. It is a simple yet unwavering acceptance of their parents' word. Our response to Christ is similar. We make a conscious decision to participate in the Spirit-directed process of confession and belief based on the surety of His promises. *Heart faith involves a voluntary state of mind, but it is essentially an act of the will.*

Paul puts it this way: "Faith comes by hearing, and hearing by the word of God" (Rom. 10:17, NKJV). The unshakable nature of the Word of Christ gives us the confidence we need to confess and believe. This idea is essential for transformation.

God is able to transform our lives by replacing hesitation with bold confidence built off a maturing belief in the sure promises of God. To see transformation in our heart and lives, our faith must rest in the Word of God.

Putting your faith completely in the Word of God is also critical to breaking the tendency of self-righteousness. In Romans 10:6–7 Paul warns us against the innate self-deception that human attempts are able to earn righteousness based on our own efforts. Paul writes, "'Do not say in your heart, "Who will ascend into heaven?"'" (that is, to bring Christ down), 'or "Who will descend into the abyss?"'" (that is, to bring Christ up from the dead)." Here, Paul urges against attempting to make our own way, even to Christ. All our seemingly pious attempts to demonstrate our own righteousness only demonstrate active unbelief.

Notice the thought-process taking place in this passage: "'Who will ascend into heaven?'… 'Who will descend into the abyss?'" The idea of scaling the heights or plumbing the depths to find Christ sounds noble, even holy. However, it is really unbelief masked in the form of self-righteousness. This kind of thinking actually distances us from Christ and His kingdom. It inhibits our ability to participate in heaven's plan of righteousness and all God's benefits connected with it.

A transformed heart eliminates all former humanistic thinking. It embraces Christ on Christ's terms because of a sure confidence in the faithfulness of His Word. We are moved from worthless self-effort to glorious Christ-commitment, resulting in victorious ways of living.

The transformation internally enables us to finally lay our will at the feet of Jesus. In doing so we allow God to fulfill His promises in our life. *Christ-commitment helps us realize our position of righteousness and moves us to a place spiritually where we can receive heaven's blessings.*

We see a small glimpse of what this way of life looks like in Romans 10:11 (NASU):

> For the Scripture says, "WHOEVER BELIEVES IN HIM WILL NOT BE DISAPPOINTED."

Now, this verse is not saying that Christians will never be disappointed in the circumstances of life. There are going to be times when others will let us down and when situations are difficult. What the Bible is promising is that God will keep His side of the covenant. Those who call on Him will be saved and will be eternally saved by Christ's righteousness.

The transformation only Christ can produce in our heart will prevent eternal disappointment. We will not be put to shame in this life or in the one to come. *Our thought patterns are transformed; no longer are we fearful or insecure.* Condemnation and shame are removed from our spiritual experience. Self-hatred and anxiety were dealt with and exterminated with a deathblow. Our minds are cleared from all this demonic debris so that we can truly fix our thoughts on Jesus, "the apostle and high priest of our confession" (Heb. 3:1).

His perfect sacrifice of Himself on the cross guarantees that if we will respond by faith and confession we will experience the vital heart transformation needed for a renewed life. This is intense as well as spiritually powerful. Our confession of faith combined with His gift of righteousness is transformative on every level.

Think big—believe!

GO-BIG QUESTIONS

1. A new heart is a _____.

2. Heart faith involves a _____, but it is essentially an act of the will.

3. Our thought patterns are transformed; no longer are we
    _____ or _____.

4. How can you implement faith into your words? Share your
    thoughts below.

_____

_____

_____

THE POWER OF FAITH

ONE OF THE enemy's favorite diversions once we make the decision to believe the good news is intimidation. Satan's mission of destruction can still occur. He tries to be a convincing bully to keep the believer from making any forward strides in his or her walk with God.

Paul, of all men, certainly knew the weight of social and spiritual pressure to keep his faith to himself. He was beaten, imprisoned, mocked, scorned, and ridiculed for his faith. Imagine the thoughts that must have bombarded his mind as the enemy attempted to shut down the force of the transformation that had taken root inside his heart.

Paul had to deal with this intimidation directly. How? He boldly proclaims his response in the opening chapter of the Book of Romans. Using a very personal confession, he states his position for all generations to follow.

> For I am not ashamed of the gospel, *because it is the power of God that brings salvation to everyone who believes:* first to the Jew, then to the Gentile. For in the gospel the righteousness of God is revealed—a righteousness that is by faith from first to last, just as it is written: "The righteous will live by faith."
> —ROMANS 1:16–17, NIV, EMPHASIS ADDED

Notice the connection between the power of God unto salvation, faith, and his bold confession. Faith for salvation is a necessary component in triumphing over intimidation. We refuse to be cowed by the enemy. Faith is our weapon. Faith accesses the power of God to dispel the gloomy haze of satanic scare tactics.

Paul goes on to remind us that the power of God is available for anyone, anywhere. There are no geographical restrictions to the power released through sincere faith. God's righteousness is no longer hidden. Jews and Gentiles alike can experience the glorious freedom of righteousness by faith. It is evident—clearly articulated in the gospel—that Jesus Christ makes sinners righteous by His death and resurrection. The glorious gospel of Jesus Christ conveys God's grace to the sinner.

Paul knew this as clearly as anyone. Religion and legalism had turned him into a murderer and bully. He persecuted Christians for pleasure, hardening his heart to the simplicity of the gospel message. Then, in only a moment, the power of faith transformed him from the inside out. His sins were forgiven, and he was given a new heart. Surely, if Christ could accomplish this for Paul then the power of God could be effective for all nations. No wonder the enemy wanted to shut him down. Paul had gone from a murderous thinker to a missional thinker!

The gospel is a global message releasing the kingdom of God in every nation. Faith has power not only for regeneration but also for ongoing proclamation. *Faith affects our thoughts, moving us from intimidation to consecration to action.*

I can almost see Paul, his words exploding from this mind-set: "I will not be ashamed, devil! The power of God has been released in my life through my response of faith to the gospel, and I'm going to articulate the power of faith so clearly and so succinctly that anyone, anywhere, who reads this letter will have the same experience!"

An illustration of the power of faith was shown in my early ministry involvement in the great nation of Russia. It was March of 1991, and Russia was grappling with the void caused by the ongoing collapse of communism.

Two other ministers and I were on our way to speak at a Russian high school and distribute the Book of Hope. It was to be the first time Americans had visited this school. Additionally, it was to be the first time the gospel would be proclaimed in this area in many decades.

The principal had organized a forty-five-minute assembly, during which I would be given twenty to thirty minutes to speak. In the remaining time our team would be able to answer questions from the students and teachers. Beforehand, our young interpreter, who was a graduate of that school, and I took the principal aside to discuss the assembly. I mentioned that I would be talking about Jesus Christ and asked if it would be possible to invite students to receive Christ following the message. Her answer almost unraveled me: "Do whatever you want. You are in Russia. You are free."

As I began speaking to the crowd, I explained that we were there to give them the gift of the Book of Hope, scriptures from the Word of God harmonized to help them know about the life of Christ. I shared about Christ's death on the cross for our sin, followed by His resurrection. He was not dead but alive. He was present to transform their lives by forgiving sin and giving them a relationship with God.

When I gave the invitation—"Who wants to receive this free gift? Raise your hand"—hands went up everywhere with excitement.

Right then, to my right, about nine young men starting booing. Tension quickly filled the air. My mouth became dry, and my hands began to perspire. I asked everyone who lifted their hand to stand up. No one responded. The nine young men seemed very pleased with this result. Their laughter was insulting!

I asked my interpreter if she would ask one more time for anyone who wanted to receive life to stand and receive Jesus as their Savior. She was hesitant and asked if it was really necessary. "Please just ask one more time," I remarked. "Is there anyone who wants to receive Jesus as their Savior? Please stand up."

Toward the back of the room one young man very slowly began to stand. One of the nine motioned with his hands for him to sit down. Yet, he remained standing! "*Nyet*," the Russian word for no, thundered from the mockers. The young man stood up even taller. Then two young ladies on the front row also stood up, followed by the entire front row. The power of the Holy Spirit drew these young hearts open until everyone was standing but the nine.

My interpreter's eyes were filled with tears. "Are you alright?" I asked.

"I have never seen such courage," she responded. "May I receive Jesus today also?"

I laughed with joy. "Certainly! We will all pray together!"

Tears filled my eyes as I witnessed the courage of this young man's heart before his teachers, friends, and classmates as I led the school in the sinner's pray that day. This young man had unlocked the secret power of faith. He had experienced the power of faith by surrendering his life to Jesus.

Yes, the gospel is powerful stuff! Think big! Faith releases the power of God to break intimidation!

Think big—believe!

GO-BIG QUESTIONS

1. It is the _____ that brings salvation to everyone who _____.

2. The power of God is available for _____.

3. _____ affects the thoughts of a man, moving him from intimidation to consecration to action.

4. What does the Bible have to say about the areas of your life you are intimidated in? Share your thoughts below.

_____

_____

_____

DAY 5
TO BELIEVE OR NOT TO BELIEVE

EVERYONE HAS FAITH in something, even if that something is nothing. Whether you have faith in something or faith in nothing, either requires faith. What you believe is where your faith is formed. The accumulation of knowledge through experience and study shapes our beliefs, and our beliefs form the foundation for faith. In other words, faith exists because of beliefs.

Faith is a substance that requires an ignition of beliefs. We are active participants in faith when we make the decision to believe. In literature, conversation, or even music, the meaning of each word being used has a profound effect on the understanding of the concept being communicated.

The best way to understand what an author is saying is to learn the definitions of the term in various contexts. The Hebrew word for "believe" is 'aman, which comes from a root meaning "to prop or to support."[1] Second Kings 18:16 uses 'aman to highlight the "support or stability of the doorpost" of the temple.[2]

> At this time Hezekiah king of Judah stripped off the gold with which he had covered the doors and doorpost of the temple of the LORD, and gave it to the king of Assyria.
> —2 KINGS 18:16, NIV

Hezekiah had rebelled against the king of Assyria. His rebellion failed, and he needed to buy protection, so he stripped the doorposts. The main point here seems to be that the doorposts were stripped of their value because the people of God had relied on their own ingenuity; they no longer valued God. As their faith eroded, the pillars supporting the house of God were stripped of their value because of a deliberate decision not to believe in God, His protection and deliverance.

In Exodus 17:11, the word is used to describe the support given by Aaron and Hur to Moses.[3] As long as Moses's hands remained elevated, there would be victory in the battlefield below. When he became fatigued, Aaron and Hur supported his hands. The Hebrew word *emunah* (derived from *'aman*) conveys the idea of holding something steady, e.g., Moses's hands. The imagery is powerful: What we believe determines our resources and our relationships. God is our source, but people are our resource. Faith ensures that God's provision can flow to us through God's people around us.

One scholar notes that "the 'first use' of a word in Scripture is often very significant, as it establishes the primary or most significant meaning" for that word.[4] *'Aman* first appears in Genesis 15:6 in the Abraham narrative. This general principle is true in the Spirit's inspired use of *'aman* in Genesis 15:6: "[Abraham] believed in the LORD, and he counted it to him as righteousness."

Here the use of *believe* is a verbal form of *'aman*. Its use "in this passage indicates that Abram did not just give mental assent to God's promise (Gen. 15:5) but that he relied on that promise and made a personal commitment to it. In other words, Abram's faith was not only cognitive (the mental act of acquiring knowledge) but also…[personally transformational], for he believed God's word of promise,"[5] even to the extent of surrendering the entire direction of His life.

He chose to believe and depend on God. For the first time in Scripture, faith and righteousness appear together. Hebrews 11:8 continues this idea: "By faith Abraham obeyed when he was called to go out to a place that he was to receive as an inheritance. And he went out, not knowing where he was going."

Faith is the root that produces the fruit of obedience. Obedience is a sign that faith is an authentic, saving faith that leads to righteousness. It is not just some sort of mental assent! Our world is full of people who mentally assent to the basic tenets of the Christian faith. This is never enough! We are called to know His righteousness!

To think like Jesus we must allow faith to move us far beyond a place of mental acceptance. Without this kind of commitment we will not have the perseverance necessary to endure the trials of this life. The Abraham story illustrates this principle well. Hebrews 11:17–19 reveals the depth of Abraham's faith, which led to the ultimate act of obedience—the sacrificing of Isaac on the altar.

> By faith Abraham, when he was tested, offered up Isaac, and he who had received the promises was in the act of offering up his only son, of whom it was said, "Through Isaac shall your offspring be named." He considered that God was able even to raise him from the dead, from which, figuratively speaking, he did receive him back.

The emotional anguish Abraham must have experienced in this moment is indescribable. His decision to believe was being fully tested. Personal faith would require the ultimate personal commitment of radical obedience. Would he believe God, even when it made no sense? Would he trust the promises of God when his mind argued against him? He committed his soul to the faithfulness of God.

Abraham's faith was serious. It determined life or death, not only for Isaac but also for the future of the seed God had promised him. The future of the plan of redemption was on the line. His faith had serious ramifications. Yes, faith is powerful, transformational stuff.

Paul's use of Genesis 15:6 in Romans 4:3, Romans 4:9, Romans 4:22, and Galatians 3:6 demonstrates that this Old Testament verse is foundational for our understanding of what it means to believe in God's faithfulness today. *When we choose to believe, even in the face of overwhelming challenges and trials, we are standing on the faithfulness of God and His Word.* Perseverance makes our belief become sight.

Considering that *amen* ("truly, it is certain") is derived from *'aman*, it is as if Abraham heard God's promise in Genesis 15:5 and said, "Amen! God is faithful to His promises, and I will believe, no matter what."[6] This required tremendous perseverance. His decision to believe opened his eyes to another realm of possibility—the certainty of God's promise.

Interestingly, Jesus repeatedly used the same Hebrew word, *amen* ("truly"), to express the trustworthiness and abiding certainty of His sayings. When we believe, we are empowered to think on a totally different plane of possibility. The promises of God become our substance and support in the face of every trial.

Charles Spurgeon connects this idea of endurance in faith and seeing the promises of God in his sermon on "Believing to See." He says:

> Oh, let us go on, we who are younger, who have scarcely begun the voyage, knowing that all is well! Storms may toss us about. Waves may dash against our hull. The billows may seem as if about to swallow us up. But our fathers have gained the beach. Their ships, like those of Columbus, are drawn up on yonder shore. They are safe and blessed. Hark! We can almost hear their song. Their, 'Hallelujah, hallelujah, hallelujah, for the Lord God Omnipotent reigns!" might almost be heard even here, were not this earth so full of noise—were not the whirl of the wheels of business so incessant. Let us, then, O let us believe to see, and we shall soon see it and glorify Him who taught us so to believe.[7]

To believe is to see the promises of God! To believe is to enter into a place of certainty in God's commitment to His Word. To believe is the power to endure the storm. To believe is the unseen capacity to persevere through every trial. This confidence of faith elevates our thinking to see by the eyes of the Spirit instead of the eyes of circumstance.

Think big—believe!

Go-Big Questions

1. _____ is the root that produces fruit
   of _____.

2. To think like Jesus we must allow _____.

3. When we choose to _____ we are standing
   on _____.

4. Why is faith important? Share your thoughts below.

_____

_____

_____

DAY 6
BELIEF AND THE FOUNDATION OF COVENANT

FAITH IS A substance according to Hebrews 11. In the previous chapter we discussed how the substance of faith is needed in the decision to believe. The expression of the substance of faith always requires the verb *believe*. Unfortunately, the modern usage of the word *believe* lacks a critical aspect of the original substance and meaning of the Hebrew word *'aman*. *This missing component is the important concept of covenant.*

In modern culture we use the expression "I believe you" somewhat flippantly. What we mean by this phrase is that we accept what is being said. This would have very little commitment beyond acceptance or agreement. Scripturally speaking, belief definitely includes this idea of agreement.

In fact, when Paul instructs the Roman believers that they are to profess with the mouth by faith in order to be saved, the Greek word that he uses for "profess" is *homologeo*.[1] Its meaning is "to speak the same thing" or "be in agreement and accord with someone." This agrees well with the modern idea of *believe*. Yet, this isn't enough. Belief is so much deeper.

Chuck Swindoll observes in *Understanding Christian Theology* that:

> Tragically, many people are convinced that it doesn't really matter what you believe, so long as you are sincere. This reminds me of a *Peanuts* cartoon in which Charlie Brown is returning from a disastrous baseball game. The caption read, "174 to nothing! How could we lose when we were so sincere?" The reality is, Charlie Brown, it takes more than sincerity to win the game of life. Many people are sincere about their beliefs, but they are sincerely wrong![2]

Clearly, mental assent is no guarantee of victory in this life. There is a much deeper aspect of *believe* involving covenant. In order to better understand this idea, we need to examine Paul's

23

conception of *believe*. In 2 Timothy 1:12, Paul gives us another glimpse of the word. He offers his spiritual son some profound insight about the true nature of faith.

> [For this reason] I also suffer these things: nevertheless I am not ashamed: for I know whom I have believed, and am persuaded that He is able to keep what I have committed unto him [until that day]. (KJV)

Interestingly, Paul is again describing one of the many reasons for his refusal to be ashamed for believing the gospel. In the previous chapter we looked at the power of God being released by faith for salvation. Here in his communication with Timothy he offers another reason: he knows whom he has believed.

This knowledge has produced a persuasion or conviction deep inside his heart. *He knows that Christ is able to keep the sacred trust of the transformation activated in his new heart through the gospel.* So what is Paul telling us about the action of believing?

The key to understanding the word *believe* is better insight into the word *know*. We first see it appear in the Old Testament Book of Genesis. Within the first four chapters of the Bible's opening pages we see the word *know* appear in the context of relationship.

> And Adam knew Eve his wife; and she conceived, and bare Cain, and said, I have gotten a man from the LORD.
>
> —GENESIS 4:1, KJV

Clearly, this verse is describing a very personal, intimate relationship between man and wife. *Know* correlates to the concept of covenant. *To believe is to be connected to covenant. This is the foundation for a victorious, overcoming life.*

The first time the word appears in the New Testament is in Luke 1:34. This time around it is being used as evidence for a lack of intimate relationship: "Then Mary said to the angel, 'How can this be, since I do not know a man?'" (NKJV). Mary is astonished at the angel's pronouncement that she will be with child. Humanly speaking, Mary and Joseph hadn't known each other, so a child was quite out of the picture. There had been no covenant, so how could there be a child?

In Scripture, then, this idea of *know* describes the covenant relationship between a man and a woman in marriage based on trust, surrender, and intimacy, with the potential of giving birth to a child. A man and woman forsake their past, their families, and all other loves in order to enter into this kind of covenant. Obviously, this goes much deeper than the idea of mere acceptance. This is personal. This is intimate. *This level of belief is costly, possessing the power for reproduction. It leads to victory.*

Paul is saying that he has entered into a covenant relationship based on faith where he will forsake all other gods. From this day forward everything inside of him will be about Jesus. He will seek relationship with Jesus above all other pursuits. He will pursue heaven's purposes. He will embrace the kingdom. He will think the thoughts of Christ. This is the true picture of *believe*. Sadly, it is an idea very foreign to many Christians today.

This definition of *believe* connects the difference between Christ being Savior and Christ being Lord. We have a generation that is comfortable with Christ as Savior. Sin produces enough pain in this world to warrant a Savior. Forgiveness is a very desirable concept. So this message is rather easy to embrace.

However, this is only the first step in our relationship with God. He desires something so much deeper than just the forgiveness of our sins; He wants to reign in our heart. *This is the lordship aspect of His triumph on the cross. He wants to be fully in control of our life.*

If Jesus is not your Lord, He is not your Savior. Many people acknowledge that Jesus is both the Son of God and Lord of the universe. Paul makes it clear in Romans 10, where he tells us, "If you confess with your mouth that Jesus is Lord and believe in your heart that God raised him from the dead, you will be saved" (v. 9).

He is speaking of the deep, personal, abiding conviction that will publicly confess Jesus as Lord, a conviction that will confess that Jesus is the believer's own sovereign, ruling Lord, in whom alone he trusts for salvation and to whom he submits. To believe is to embrace Christ's lordship. Not to believe is to reject Christ's lordship. This belief arises from a transformed heart that has experienced the power of active faith.

The old expression is true: if Jesus is not Lord of all, then He is not Lord at all. *This is the essence of covenant—total abandonment to the lordship of Christ.* When Jesus is fully Lord we experience the genuine power of salvation in our lives. We choose to believe in our hearts and confess with our mouths to experience God's power. Think big by making Jesus the Lord of every aspect of your life!

GO-BIG QUESTIONS

1. According to Hebrews 11, faith is a _____.

2. The key to understanding the word *believe* is better described using the word _____.

3. Not to _____ is to reject Christ's _____.

4. How did your understanding of belief change after reading this chapter? Share your thoughts below.

_____

_____

_____

BELIEF AND THE EXPERIENCE OF GLORY

W HEN WE MAKE the choice to believe God He gives us a new heart and new mind. We have explored this glorious truth together. Believing in Jesus Christ initiates an internal supernatural transformation. As glorious as a new heart is in the life of the believer, God has an even higher purpose in regeneration. Being born again is glorious indeed. Yet, it is just the starting point for heaven's ultimate purpose.

Our new heart has glorious capacity now that it has been made alive to the purposes of God. In the glory of new birth, our heart is cleaned out. All the old tenants are given eviction notices so that Jesus can take up residence! Paul describes this process in Colossians 1:27: "To them God chose to make known how great among the Gentiles are the riches of the glory of this mystery, which is Christ in you, the hope of glory." Did you catch that? Christ is in you. If this is really true—that the Son of the living God resides inside of believers—then where can we find Him? In our renewed heart! Jesus lives inside of us.

In the New Testament we see many different powerful thoughts concerning God and His position toward believers. First of all, we see that *God is with us*. This is the launching point of the Gospels and the heart of the Christmas message. In a manger, Emmanuel, "God is with us," is born to end seven hundred–plus years of anticipation for the Messiah. Jesus demonstrates that He is both the Son of God and the Son of Man.

Secondly, we see that *God is for us*. Paul makes this clear in Romans 8:31: "If God is for us, then who can be against us?" As someone once remarked, God plus one always makes a majority. When God stands with us we always gain the victory!

The third thought is that *God is in us*. Most Bible commentaries believe that Colossians 1:27 is the foundational scripture for Paul's entire ministry:

> To them God chose to make known how great among the Gentiles are the riches of the glory of

this mystery, which is Christ in you, the hope of
glory.

Interestingly, we don't know if Paul ever preached in
Colossae. We know that there were three main churches in the
region. The Colossian church was the least known of the three.
Few had heard of this obscure group of believers.

Yet, in writing to a church that almost no one knew existed,
Paul develops four profound and prolific chapters on the glory
of the Godhead. It is a power-packed letter. His argument to
the insignificant believer—insignificant, at least, according to
this world's standards—is that Christ resides inside of him or
her. *In God's mind this means that there are no unimportant
people or places. Every life matters. Every heart has eternal
significance.*

Paul wants to remind the believers of the mystery that
instills them with eternal value. What is the mystery? This
mystery is that the prophetic anticipation of the Messiah is no
longer a mystery. *Christ, the Messiah, is now alive in the hearts
of believers, instilling them with the hope of glory.*

As Messiah, Jesus has made the kingdom of God a reality.
The kingdom is no longer an ethereal theological hope with no
concrete substance. Instead, it is a living entity inaugurated by
Jesus, the messianic King, in the hearts of normal people like
you and me.

It's so monumental, and yet it's possible to miss it entirely.
So, Paul calls the attention of the church to focus, fix, and
fasten their eyes on Christ Jesus. He knows that whatever
gets our attention gets us. This is a law of the mind. Children
understand it. If they can get mama's attention, then they can
get mama. What we focus on captivates our thought patterns.
*Jesus-thinkers are people who have learned to fix their attention
on the hope of glory emanating from inside their hearts.*

Before going any farther, let me share a prophetic insight
the Lord revealed to me a couple of years ago. In my spirit I
have seen a supernatural season of God's blessing rising over
the people of God. It is a prophetic indicator of God's goodness
and unmerited favor.

This season will prepare His people for the coming cataclysmic crisis on Planet Earth. Tough times are coming to this nation, as well as to this world. The people of God will be prepared because they will learn their identity as being residences of Christ the Messiah. We will invade, influence, and impact this generation. God is now raising up a people that understand the fact that church is not about four walls. *It is about the ministry of the Holy Spirit, according to my friend Michael Tyler: "Bring people into the kingdom of God, and then bring the kingdom of God into the people."*

What do I mean by that? Let's say that your residence is in the United States of America. Just because someone lives in the United States of America doesn't mean that the United States of America lives inside of them. As such, the critical revelation that must come in this hour to the body of Christ is that Christ the King is living inside our hearts.

Our challenge is to believe that Christ lives in us. We often miss this idea totally. We ask questions like, Why would Jesus want to live inside of us? I believe this question can be answered by touching on heaven's priorities.

Christ is in us, the hope of glory. What is heaven's solution for the troubles of this sin-cursed world? It's the glory of God! His glory is the answer to every human sorrow and woe. This glory now resides in His people. *His desire is for the church to release His glory into this generation.*

Several years ago I met a merchant in the streets of Moscow selling a beautifully ornate lacquer box. I asked him how much it was. He didn't seem to understand, so I asked again through my interpreter. The merchant wanted the equivalent of one hundred dollars. I wasn't ready to spend one hundred dollars. I asked him if he had a box that was cheaper.

The merchant immediately reduced the price to eighty dollars. I told him that it was worth one hundred dollars because it was so beautiful; I just didn't want to spend that much. He wanted to know why not. I told him that it was for my mother-in-law. We both laughed. I told him that I would look for a twenty-dollar box. The merchant held up the original box again and asked me how much I would give him for it. I told him that

I would buy it for twenty-five dollars. Suddenly, in perfect English, he responded, "Show me the money."

There is a crisis in the world. The crisis can be best described in the phrase "show me the money." This phrase affects the mind-set of both the church and the world. Materialism has consumed us and captivated us. Please understand that I'm not against money, but money does not produce inner transformation. Money can't fix the problems of this world. We don't need the power of money in the church; we need the power of God again. We don't need more gold; we need more glory. *Our mind-set needs to be changed back to the necessity of seeing Christ revealed through His people.*

Thinking big demands the glory of God demonstrated through our heart and life.

GO-BIG QUESTIONS

1. _____ is only just the starting point for heaven's ultimate purpose for our life.

2. In God's mind there are no _____ people or places.

3. As Messiah, Jesus made _____ a reality.

4. How can you make adjustments in your life to depend on God more than money? Share your thoughts below.

_____

_____

_____

DAY 8
BELIEF AND SURRENDER

How can we have a believing heart that releases Christ's glory into this sin-cursed world? How can our heart be made true and pure in order to reveal this hidden mystery that resides inside of us?

These are tremendously important questions. Much of the church has slipped into empty formality and rigid religiosity. The vibrancy and life of the Spirit seems distant except during special meetings or occasions. Surely, God's glory isn't seasonal. This heavenly deposit in our heart has no expiration date or dimmer switch on God's end. *We must activate His glory by surrender.*

His glory is still the critical need of our day. By *glory*, I mean the weighty, heavy presence of God. It comes from the Hebrew word *kavod,* which means "heaviness" or "weight."[1] In fact, when the *kavod* showed up during the dedication of the temple, the priests were unable to minister: "So that the priests could not stand to minister because of the cloud, for the glory of the LORD filled the house of God" (2 Chron. 5:14). The glory was so weighty that the ministers of the Lord couldn't even stand up. God's presence had filled the house as they surrendered to His moving!

Kavod is used in the Old Testament over two hundred times.[2] Sometimes Scripture records it being visibly manifested, as in Exodus 40:34: "Then the cloud covered the tent of meeting, and the glory of the LORD filled the tabernacle." Here, the glory manifests as a cloud. At other times it looked like fire. Yet, whether it was actually seen or not, it could always be felt. God's weighty presence is tangible and palpable (intense) when present.

We go back to Paul's foundational scripture in Colossians 1:27: "To them God chose to make known how great among the Gentiles are the riches of the glory of this mystery, which is Christ in you, the hope of glory." God is revealing a powerful secret or mystery to the Colossian saints, as well as to saints everywhere: *God's glory now resides in the hearts of both*

31

Gentiles and Jews! Imagine the impact this statement must have had for the early church struggling to find its identity. The glory of God had been exclusively a Jewish reality up to this point in history. The Old Testament scriptures detailing the glory of God almost invariably connect this special promise to the Jewish nation walking under the Abrahamic covenant. God Himself made a special promise in Exodus, "Then I will take you for My people, and I will be your God; and you shall know that I am the LORD your God, who redeemed you and brought you out from under the burdens of the Egyptians" (Exod. 6:7, AMP). The Jewish nation was a chosen people. God was their God. His glory was the distinction of divine selection of this group of people.

In Exodus 33 Moses uses this very argument in his prayer to the Lord concerning Israel. Without God's presence in the midst of His people, nothing else would distinguish them from the other people groups and deities on the earth. Moses pleaded for the ongoing demonstration of the glory of God. He refused to continue leading the Jewish people without holy glory and divine presence.

Paul tells us that the glory is now available to each and every believer. The presence of God is no longer a Jewish monopoly. Even more incredibly, Paul tells the Colossians that His glory is now available on an ongoing measure. Where would we expect God to deposit such a magnificent treasure? A glorious palace? An ornate tabernacle? No, God says the mystery is that He has chosen the most precious place of all—the human heart.

God isn't bringing His glory into us to occupy our old heart though. This is because our old heart is so dead, so empty, and so barren that God can't use it. Ezekiel tells us that God has to put a new heart in us (Ezek. 36:26). When we believe in Jesus we are coming to God and asking Him to take out all of who we are at the core of who we are in exchange for the promise of the deposit of His glory.

God reaches in to take out the old nature. What we sometimes don't realize is that when we are asking for a new heart we are in fact asking for His heart. And the Father's heart is always for His glory! Hebrews ties the idea of God's glory and the Son of God together beautifully: "He [Jesus] is the radiance of the glory of God and the exact imprint of His nature" (Heb. 1:3). Jesus Christ is the fullest expression of God's glory! No wonder Paul can make the Spirit-inspired assertion that the hope of glory now resides inside each and every believer. Christ has our heart.

The church of Jesus Christ globally is being reminded of the necessity of God's glory being revealed again in our generation. We must have the manifest presence of God moving in our midst. His weighty presence will accomplish more than we can ever hope to with our limited abilities and resources. One moment in His presence still sets captives free. *His glory still brings healing to the sick and oppressed.*

So what is the secret to experiencing His glory in our midst in this generation? Simply this: *God must have our heart— wholly and unreservedly.* The glory of God in the person of Christ lives inside the believer's heart through faith. His glory is already deposited in His people. Our challenge then is to let it out by giving God full access to our heart.

Many believers have reserve areas of their hearts that are off limits to Jesus and His purposes. This touches on the idea of lordship again, which we have already examined. It's a life of percentages: partial access to God and partial control for us. Living this kind of life is one of compromise impeding the flow of God's glory in and through us.

This is an hour for wholehearted surrender by believing. *The world needs the deposit of glory stored in our heart.* Will Jesus have full access to these deepest recesses in our hearts?

Go-Big Questions

1. Many in the *modern* church have slipped into _____ and _____.

2. God reaches in to take out the old nature of our _____ heart and _____ it with a new, clean _____.

3. God must have our heart _____,
   _____, and with no _____.

4. How can you take initiative in gaining more intimacy
   with God? Share your thoughts below.

_____

_____

_____

BELIEF AND DIRECTION

To BELIEVE WITHOUT direction is to remove the banks of a river. The end result is that we become a swamp. The banks keep the water channeled in a specific direction. The river has force and momentum. A swamp, by contrast, is stagnant and foul. The water in it usually has a funny color and strange smell.

Many people want to believe in God, but they have no direction. They have no destiny and no purpose. They just move around like a cesspool full of junk. They swirl around with no forward momentum. Life feels purposeless. There's a stink—a contamination of the heart and spirit. Obviously, this is not God's plan or purpose for our lives. Confusion, stagnancy, and uncertainty are not heaven's purpose.

The key idea here is this: believing is receiving. What is the best way to keep our heart directional and free from stagnation? We must receive from the Spirit of God by faith. This is an ongoing endeavor. We are called to receive from heaven on a continual basis. What is faith but the response of receiving unseen revelation? *For our faith to remain vibrant we must remain in a posture of reception.*

Many Christians are comfortable with this idea as it relates to the initial act of regeneration. Jesus knocks on the door of our heart. We open the door through repentance and faith. He enters to cleanse us and give us a new heart and His mind. We experience the renewal of our thinking and motivation. Jesus becomes our Savior because we have received Him. Yet, it must never stop there with one encounter at an altar.

The activity of the Spirit doesn't stop there. It is ongoing in nature. *Only when we adopt a heart posture of reception can we experience the river of the Spirit flowing inside of us.* This is critical to keep our heart out of the swamp of sin and selfishness. The work of the Spirit of God occurs in the heart. As such, it is in the heart that the Spirit leads and guides us. This is the real nature of divine direction.

Imagine a roaring river of life and vitality flowing through your heart, leading your life toward a sure and appointed destination. It's easy to find your direction because the force and current of the river move you toward a specific place. Now contrast this image with a swamp. There is sludge up to your ankles and water to your knees. It's just sitting there with no motion or movement. In order to get anywhere a traveler would have to expend lots of energy trudging through the muck. Such a trek would probably demand hours, if not days, to get across.

What a contrast in images! The Spirit of God flows through our heart, moving us toward the purposes of God. It's not always safe, but it is glorious. *He leads. He moves. He directs. It's His energy and His action. We follow. We flow. We respond. We receive.*

There are two important ideas here for keeping our heart full of direction. The first is revelation through the Word of God.

We have God's gracious offer of salvation in Christ and the provision of righteousness by faith in His Word. God opens our heart and speaks faith into our heart by His written Word. We see this clearly in Romans 10:17: "So then faith comes by hearing, and hearing by the word of God" (NKJV). *God builds faith in the heart through our receiving, believing, and obeying the Word of God.*

The Word is vitally important in maintaining spiritual momentum and ultimate direction. As our heart is exposed to the revelation of the Word of God we are strengthened with new measures of faith!

We must continually allow our heart to be strengthened and built up with faith. In terms of direction this is important because God's ways often don't make sense to our human thinking. His thoughts are not our thoughts, and His ways are not our ways (Isa. 55:8). This is not a rebuke to make us hopeless and despondent in our capacity to determine heaven's direction for our life. Rather, this is an appeal for us to change our thinking patterns by embracing heaven's thoughts even when it doesn't make sense. (See Isaiah 55:7, where humanity is called to abandon their sinful thoughts.) *The only way that we can have this kind of trust to embrace God's thinking for our lives is to build up our faith through the Word.*

I would suggest that the Word is the raft that we use to float on in the river of God. It keeps us above the flood. It keeps us headed in the right direction. Too many people are trying to fight the direction of the Lord and the flow of the river of heaven through their hearts because they are ignorant of God's thoughts.

The second important idea is motivation by the Spirit. Let's be honest; sometimes God's direction is difficult. Just ask Abraham, called to leave Ur and go to an unidentified place. Or ask Daniel in the lion's den or the three Hebrew children in the fiery furnace. His direction in our heart can be challenging. *At this critical juncture we need obedience, and obedience is much easier when we have the motivation of heaven to obey.*

It's one thing to think God's thoughts and understand His direction. It's another thing entirely to receive the motivation that we need to obey effortlessly. Is such a thing possible? Yes, I believe it is. God's will for our lives requires both direction and volition.

> If you are willing and obedient, you will eat the good things of the land.
>
> —ISAIAH 1:19, NIV

His Spirit produces an attitude of obedience. Thinking God's thoughts with God's motivation inspires us to obedience.

God's Spirit works inside of us to give us the motivation that we so desperately need in order to pursue God's direction for our lives. Simple faith, combined with the Spirit's motivation, ensures that we will stay true to heaven's direction. Both are completely available to the open heart! We can receive the direction necessary to accomplish our calling.

Think big! Think God's thoughts. Pursue heaven's direction as His Spirit flows through your heart.

GO-BIG QUESTIONS

1. To believe without direction is like removing the
   _____ of a river.

2. Believing is _____.

3. The _____ is vitally important in maintaining
   spiritual momentum and ultimate _____.

4. Are you willing to be obedient to God's calling on your
   life? Share your thoughts below.

   _____

   _____

   _____

DAY 10
BELIEF AND A WORD-FILLED HEART

ONE OF MY favorite expressions is "Believe for things so big that if God doesn't show up then we aren't going to make it." This statement challenges my faith level. After all, who wants to live a mediocre, half-hearted life for God? We want to live in such way that it will only make sense in the light of eternity. Yet, this statement is much easier said than done, because our heart quickly reverts back to small-minded faith. *Faith is so critically important to living a life of significance for God and His kingdom.*

The dimension in our heart is staggering. It is bigger than our head. It is the connection to the unseen world. Our heart can see things that our mind can't see or perceive. The mind has limitations and barriers that our heart doesn't deal with. Our mind has barriers and baggage. We can be the smartest person in the world yet still have limitations in our thinking. Much of this has to do with past experiences and interactions. We allow our heart to dream of some exploit for God, only to have our mind tell us how unrealistic that would be. "You could never do that," we quickly tell ourselves.

Our mind constantly challenges us to be realistic. No wonder Paul instructs us so forcefully in Romans 12 to "be transformed by the renewing of [our]…mind. Then you will be able to test and approve what God's will is—his good, pleasing and perfect will" (v. 2, NIV). Our mind has such barriers and restrictions that it can literally argue us out of God's glorious direction. *Without a renewed mind we can miss the capacity He has placed in our heart to engage His purpose.*

Our heart doesn't have these limitations. Our heart is the bridge between the seen world and the unseen world. The enemy wants to attack the core of who we are—our heart. Satan wants to shut down our heart, but in every situation we have the capacity to demonstrate the life and power of God living inside of our heart. *The only way that this can happen is to fill our heart with the Word of God.*

The key thought here in this chapter is that believing is feeding. Imagine someone not eating a single bite of food or drinking any water for several months at the start of a year. This is not a fast for spiritual purposes; this is months and months of total neglect. What would you think about such a person? Obviously, this is imaginary, because this person would die of malnutrition. No one would forget to eat or drink for months on end. The consequences are just too terrible.

How is it that we are so smart with our stomach and yet so disconnected with our heart? Many believers are on a heart-starvation diet. No wonder our experience in God is so shallow and lackluster. Our heart is starving for the fuel necessary to believe God for great things. Faith can only live in the context of feeding.

Look at what you are reading and who your friends are, and you can easily determine what you are feeding your heart. What are we feeding on? Who is speaking to our heart? Social media? Entertainment? We have a starving generation. Many only hear the Word preached once a week during a church service. Imagine how weak we would be if we only ate once a week.

Why is it so important to feed our heart? Our heart has the ability to believe the promises of God. Our heart often tells us that we have to try things for God; then our mind will try to talk us out of it. The head can say no, but the heart can bypass the head, encouraging us to believe God and step out. This requires great faith. This kind of faith must be fed. Only then will our heart be able to believe God instead of our own limited and restricted thinking.

When a negative report comes our way, such as a disease like cancer, the head will tell us that we better put our affairs in order because time is short. The Word-filled heart, by contrast, says, "I will live and not die and declare what the Lord has done" (Ps. 118:17, author's paraphrase). The Word-filled heart will say, "I will see the goodness of the LORD in the land of the living" (Ps. 27:13, NIV).

The Word becomes the bridge that gets us between the unseen world and the seen world. This is what the enemy fears the most—a Christian who sees heaven's unseen direction and begins to implement it in his or her life. He will throw the fury of hell against such a believer with trials and temptations. This was his attack against Jesus Himself. Satan knew that Christ would implement the Father's kingdom. Three times the enemy assailed the perfect Son of God with temptation. Amazingly, Christ's response was always the same: "It is written...." (See Matthew 4:1–11.) Jesus survived the assault by possessing a Word-filled heart that had been fed on the truths of the Old Testament.

The Word-filled heart faces each and every challenge with the strength necessary to overcome the deception and discouragement of the enemy. Let us adopt the model that Christ left us. In the face of opposition our heart will respond, "Greater is He that is in me than he who lives in the world" (1 John 4:4, author's paraphrase), and, "I can do all things through [Christ]...who gives me strength" (Phil. 4:13, NIV).

When the bank account tells us that we don't have enough money, the head will tell us that we are in trouble because we have more month than money. The Word-filled heart will reply, "My God will supply all of my needs according to His glorious riches in Christ Jesus" (Phil. 4:19, author's paraphrase).

We have the power to move into every situation and release God's power through our heart when it is full of God's Word! The only thing that can stop us is our mind. This is because it is the gateway to our heart. Paul knew this. Jesus knew this. We must be transformed by the renewing of our mind. This happens by feeding our heart a steady diet of the Word of God.

Think big! Believing God for great things is possible with a Word-filled heart.

GO-BIG QUESTIONS

1. Believe for things so _____ that if God doesn't show up we aren't going to _____ it.

2. When we accept Christ into our heart we are given His
   _____ over _____.

3. When our heart is full of God's _____ we
   have the power to move into every situation and release
   God's _____!

4. What is something you can believe for in your life that is
   so big it is something only God could accomplish? Share
   your thoughts below.

_____

_____

_____

DAY 11
BELIEF AND AN OVERFLOWING HEART
*I don't want to reap from what I have sown; I
want to reap from what God has sown.*

OUR FIST IS like a heart. The heart is about the size of the human fist, so to compare the two works as a good visual illustration. Our heart is one of the strongest muscles in the body. It is a pump that deals with giving and receiving. It gives blood and receives blood, pumping over a billion times in the life of an average person. The healthier the heart, the more powerful it contracts to give blood to the rest of the body. This is measured by heartbeats per minute.

However, heart constriction leads to heart failure and a lowering of the quality of life. Similarly, mind constriction leads to memory loss and a devastated life. Spiritually, many people live a depleted life with a closed-fist mentality. *When we believe in Jesus Christ and confess Him as Lord and Savior, He will break the stingy mind-set.*

Many are controlled by the idea of insufficiency. "Not enough" is the classic idea behind this mind-set. Here are some verbs that demonstrate this form of thinking: *hoard, hold, reserve, restrict, limit, retain, protect, save,* and *keep.* It's the picture of the fist grasping on to something for dear life.

Can you imagine being married to such a person? Someone who holds on to every cent? They refuse to ever take any risks. Their tightened fists keep other people out of family affairs and relationships. They refuse to share personal thoughts, dreams, or accomplishments with others. Their time is their own, and they hoard their time from God and family. No, thank you! I praise God that my wife, Marsha, is the exact opposite—a woman who refuses to let her heart be constricted and confined like a tight fist.

By contrast, when the heart is open and full of Christ's generosity it is comparable to the open hand. Believing in Jesus releases the stranglehold of selfishness over our resources—finances, relations, and time. Have you ever spent time with givers? They inspire us also to be like-minded. They stretch our heart beyond our comfort zone. The greatest giver of all time is Jesus. He gave up His home, His comforts, His rights, His glory, His time, and ultimately, His very life. The more we allow the life of Jesus to infuse our heart, the more generous we become.

The key thought in this chapter is the idea that *believing leads to giving*. To say we believe in Jesus yet live with a closed fist is a contradiction of terms. A stingy mind-set demonstrates the exact opposite of a believing heart. Believing in Christ demands generosity.

The power of giving is in relationship to receiving. Let's return to the heart analogy. The moment that my heart sends blood coursing through my veins, more comes pouring back into the chambers of the heart. The same is true with our heart in a spiritual sense. I give, and it pumps again so that I receive. Receive. Give. Receive. Give. The two are integrally connected.

The dynamic of these two factors determine the health of our heart. When either is out of balance, then our heart stops functioning properly and eventually dies. If we adopt a mind-set that is narrow, restricted, and confined we will see things through the lens of restriction and limitation. Without an outflow in the form of giving we quickly become stagnant in our faith. God's fresh deposit in our lives always follows a fresh surrender of our heart. When we give our lives away He gives us more of Himself.

One of the primary areas where we can see this principle clearly is in finances. They are measurable and immediate. The value of finances correlates to the condition of our heart. Our money doesn't just represent us; it represents the heart of God. *Giving indicates the measure of our faith.* Jesus put it this way: "Where your treasure is, there your heart will be also" (Matt. 6:21).

This is the dynamic of giving and receiving with an overflowing heart. When the heart is full in faith, then we are able to give effortlessly. We have received something far greater than we are giving away. The priority of tithing illustrates the health of our heart. When we give we are making a declaration that God is first in our lives. Giving says that I live a life that goes beyond a life that I see with my eyes. When I give I anticipate the ongoing reception of His provision.

Beyond finances, belief in Jesus Christ requires the investment of who we are in the kingdom of God. We are God's currency in the kingdom. To state this another way: What does God use as currency in His kingdom? People. What kind of people? People whose hearts are full of faith and have adopted a mind-set of generosity. These kinds of people are overflowing with the ultimate resource—God Himself.

The beauty of an overflowing heart is found in an ongoing experience with Christ. We are prepared for vibrant service in the kingdom. The river of the Spirit flows through our heart to resource us for effective kingdom service.

Paul highlights the idea of overflowing in several places in the New Testament.

"May the God of hope fill you with all joy and peace as you trust in him, so that you may overflow with hope by the power of the Holy Spirit"(Rom. 15:13, NIV). This is an overflow of hope.

"I pray that your love will overflow more and more, and that you will keep on growing in knowledge and understanding" (Phil. 1:9, NLT). This is an overflow of love.

"Let your roots grow down into him, and let your lives be built on him. Then your faith will grow strong in the truth you were taught, and you will overflow with thankfulness" (Col. 2:7, NLT). This is the overflow of gratitude from an inflow of faith into our heart.

"And God is able to make all grace overflow to you, so that because you have enough of everything in every way at all times, you will overflow in every good work" (2 Cor. 9:8, NET). This is an overflow of grace for every good work.

The end result of a heart of faith will always be overflow in every other area of life. This is not to imply that there won't be challenges, difficulties, or even temptations. These are all a part of the human experience. *Rather, as we intentionally live a life of giving we will find that we will receive His supply of grace for every situation.* Even though we may have to walk through the valley of the shadow of death and experience the presence of our enemies around us, yet our life will overflow in God's generosity (Ps. 23).

We can never out-give God. *A mind-set of generosity coupled with an overflowing heart of love will abound in kingdom service.* Open your hand! Open your heart! Think big! Receive big!

GO-BIG QUESTIONS

1. The heart is a pump that continually utilizes
   _____ and _____.

2. We are God's currency in the _____.

3. As we intentionally live a life of giving and receiving we find that our heart never lacks _____ for every situation.

4. What areas of your life can you stretch your giving? Share your thoughts below.

_____

_____

_____

DAY 12
BELIEF AND THE ACTION OF FAITH

MOVEMENT INDICATES LIFE. Lack of movement can indicate death. If there is no action in a believer's life something is lacking. Action of the believing heart is proof that there is something happening inside. James 2:14 address this important subject: "What good is it, dear brothers and sisters, if you say you have faith but don't show it by your actions? Can that kind of faith save anyone?" (NLT). *Clearly, there is a direct spiritual correlation between action and faith.*

Actions represent our heart, our attitude, our decisions, and our motivation. Our thoughts develop our attitude. Our attitude directs our decisions. Our decisions determine our actions or destination. Our destination determines our consequences or rewards. *Everything centers on action, but it has to be the right action.*

In the Old Testament everything was also about actions. God gave Adam and Eve a promise that He would send someone to set them free from the bondage of sin. God reiterated the promise to Moses and brought the Israelites into a covenantal relationship with Him. God gave them the sacrificial system to help keep the Israelites in a pure relationship with Him. He called the Israelites to be a light to the Gentiles. But the Israelites did not comply with God's command. Time and again God sent prophets to call the Israelites back to true belief and to show it by their action of right living.

> For I desire mercy, not sacrifice, and acknowledgement of God rather than burnt offerings.
>
> —HOSEA 6:6, NIV

Instead, the Israelites tried to fulfill God's laws by passing many more laws, which bound men and women into keeping over six hundred rabbinical statutes. The Old Testament is replete with those who loved God and showed through their actions their belief and trust in God. However, the Old

Testament also shows man's heart of sin in turning from the living God to syncretistic religion and idol worship.

We can safely say that righteousness was determined by action. The action of obedience to God's Word produced commendation from God. However, man turned a covenantal relationship with God into a system characterized by rules and regulations to control actions. For many it became nothing more than systemized legalism. *Actions demonstrated compliance with the religious and legal system.*

The challenge with this system was that those in relationship with God could have correct action while possessing incorrect motivation. It was possible to have a seemingly correct external righteousness without internal righteousness. It was a mere shadow of what God envisioned in the garden.

Obviously, God was after more than robotic legalism—a form of external compliance. He desired intimacy. He longed for relationship. This would be a different system. It would be one based on a new covenant, a transformation of the heart and mind, as we have already examined in this book. It was God's means of affecting the internal realities.

In the New Testament Jesus didn't start with the "beactions"; He started with the Beatitudes. Jesus went much deeper than a mere external conformity to the age-old commands found in the Mosaic Law. "Don't do this" or "don't do that" connected to the rabbinic commands. Jesus came to place the emphasis on our thoughts. He wanted to take the discussion to a whole other dimension of the human experience. Jesus wanted to know if our thoughts and attitudes were right with God.

We see this idea clearly in the well-known Sermon on the Mount section in Matthew. Jesus began His ministry with the Beatitudes, which illustrated the necessity of heart transformation to produce kingdom motivation. These attitudes or heart postures inform our sense of being. Then He illustrates the insufficiencies of the old, external system of realities. He uses anger, adultery, and divorce to illustrate the limitations of the old covenant.

Jesus restates the demands of the Law before revealing the even more stringent requirements of the kingdom. He states that it's not enough to refrain from murder, as the Old Testament instructed. Avoiding violence would have been an acceptable action. Now, Jesus raises the bar by stating that anger is grounds for judgment. Concerning adultery, Jesus says that it is just the fruit of a far bigger root—lust. He has lifted the standards again by going deep into the human heart. Divorce is governed by the same principle of a higher standard under the new paradigm.

What is Jesus aiming at in this discourse? He is revealing the imperative of heart-level transformation. External action can be accomplished without a renewed heart. In other words, without kingdom motivation we will never be able to pursue authentic kingdom action. *Jesus wants our heart to be His heart. He wants our thoughts to be His thoughts. Only then can our actions be His actions.*

Jesus is articulating the necessity for righteous kingdom action. Yet, His argument is that kingdom action is impossible without the power of a transformed heart. *Once transformed by the Spirit of God, however, faith overflows into authentic action. The key thought here is that believing is achieving.*

Jesus gives us a glimpse of the heart attitudes necessary for kingdom action. He describes the joy of giving expression to these attitudes. Each statement in the Beatitudes is introduced with the same expression of contentment: "Blessed are...," or, "Happy are...." In each of the circumstances Jesus describes— being "poor in spirit," mourning, meekness, having a "hunger... for righteousness," and so forth—He describes the heart posture using the same term (Matt. 5:3-10). The idea is that once the heart expresses the reality of the kingdom, *faith in action will produce great joy in the life of the believer.* There is a measure of happiness that can only be experienced in the context of kingdom living.

Jesus is giving us a clear picture of the condition of the heart that is necessary for it to be moved to action by faith. He promises a special blessing with each Beatitude. The poor in spirit inherit the kingdom of heaven. Those who mourn are comforted. The meek inherit the Earth. The hungry and thirsty for righteousness are filled. The merciful receive mercy. The pure in heart see God. The peacemakers are the sons of God. The persecuted inherit the kingdom. (See Matthew 5:3–12.) In each of these instances, *blessed* is both a heart condition that produces righteous action and a consequence of walking in the footsteps of Christ.

We see from this list that faith requires action in the heart in order to be considered alive. In other words, faith is proved real by action. It is imperative that we allow our heart to be activated by faith. This will stir us to do something, to respond, to express the faith inside of us, and to experience real, God-given joy! There is a sense of God moving us to holy action as we respond to His Word. Living faith *achieves*. It is not some form of human striving. Rather, it is the natural extension of faith deposited into the heart. Achievement is not a negative thing; it's a necessary thing in the kingdom of God. It reveals the condition of faith. The end result is always glory for God.

In 2013 I conducted special youth meetings in St. Petersburg, Russia, during the week of Christmas. Close to five thousand young people participated. We had six services in three days in the freezing cold weather. More than two hundred responded to Christ as Savior with another eleven hundred or so receiving a fresh surge of faith in their lives. On the final night hundreds of young people danced all over the front of the building, experiencing the message of joy for all people. It was quite a sight to behold.

The normal, reserved Russian temperament dissolved as their hearts were moved to a place of holy action! Through the simple act of believing the message they responded immediately to God's presence in their lives. While it may seem insignificant to dance across the front of a building, I assure you that it was a huge step of faith for these young people. This is the same kind of step that we are all challenged to take regularly in our walk with Christ.

In the next section of this book we want to consider the power of faith overflowing within our heart in the form of action. This idea incorporates holy achievement. Christ wants to release glorious deeds in and through His people that will transform the world. Think big—believe! Definitely, this is important. Now let's act big—believe.

Go-Big Questions

1. There is a direct correlation between _____ and _____.

2. Everything centers on action, but it has to be the _____ action.

3. Once transformed by the Spirit of God, faith overflows into _____.

4. How can you line up your thoughts and attitudes to match Christ's? Share your thoughts below.

_____

_____

_____

BE BOLD BRAVE BRILLIANT

PART 2

ACT BIG

THE MIND OF CHRIST AND PERSONAL TRANSFORMATION

DAY 13
MOMENTUM: THE ACTION OF FAITH

CTION BEGINS IN the heart, as we understand the power of our calling in Christ. We have spent significant time developing the importance of a renewed heart in previous chapters. Now it's time to see how this plays out in the practical application of living a life of action (faith).

Momentum is a critical component of action. *The definition of* momentum *is "the impetus gained by a moving object."* It can also be defined as "the quantity of motion of a moving body measured as a product of its mass and velocity."[1] The object in question is our heart; it gives motion to our body. Faith brings the heart to life, and the inward working of the Spirit gives our heart dreams, thoughts, ideas, vision, and mission—all of which have mass in the spirit.

Scientifically, multiple actions exerted in the same direction on one particular object produce motion. When motion is accelerated through this same process we have momentum. Momentum is very hard to slow down. Just ask the avalanche that has absorbed all of the little flakes of snow on the side of the mountain. As it comes crashing down with force we would be hard pressed to stop its momentum. Yet, the real power of the avalanche is with the individual flakes of snow slowly being combined in the overall direction of the whole.

As we grow in our understanding of our calling in the kingdom of God, we quickly start gaining momentum. God's Spirit works powerfully inside of us to give our life kingdom direction and kingdom significance. *We find that little steps of obedience, combined with prayer, surrender, and the Word, are the raw ingredients for a spiritual avalanche.* Action steps to implement this inner transformation quickly produce velocity and motion. We are moving toward the high calling for our lives (Phil. 3:14).

Honestly, momentum is the key to success in life. The more motion toward a Spirit-birthed direction in the kingdom of God, the more purpose our life will carry. Momentum is the key to living a life beyond our current level of thinking. Momentum releases the thoughts of God like a flood into our minds. We find ourselves overtaken by both substance as well as motion. God is always on the move! Momentum helps us keep up with Him. We yearn for His inner working in our heart to produce external momentum.

I like to say that momentum is our God-given cry for more—more of God's love, more of God's presence, more of God's direction, more of His vision, more of His grace, more of His strength, more of His purpose in our heart and life. It's the yearning for the direction of our life, measured by action, to be meaningful and eternally significant.

I'm not saying that there aren't times when God has us pull away for a season of pruning or waiting. I certainly don't mean to imply that life has no obstacles or challenges. Indeed, suffering is a part of the Christian experience. What I am saying is that when we get the big picture of heaven's perspective, we realize that even these seasons of seeming retreat are really cumulative in their nature. They are individual action steps in our spiritual life that, when surrendered to the hands of God, ultimately fulfill a purpose much bigger than us.

Beyond this individual level I sense something bigger for the body of Christ. I already mentioned the prophetic insight the Lord has given me about His people on day 7 of this devotional. It involves a supernatural season of God's blessing rising over the people of God. It is a season to prepare God's people for the coming cataclysmic crisis on the face of Planet Earth. We are being called together to ensure that we don't squander this moment of supernatural opportunity. *We are to invade, influence, and impact our generation. I would suggest that momentum is the only way that this can become a reality!*

One of the most significant verses on momentum found in the Bible is Colossians 1:27: "Christ in you, the hope of glory." This verse describes the weight or substance of what has been deposited in the transformed heart. I'm not arguing action for action's sake. I'm talking about the presence of God giving our life the motion we need to change this world and impact this generation. This is sanctified, or holy, action. With Christ guiding our heart and our mind, we take strategic steps toward His purpose. This results in more glory to His name.

In order to get our mind more fully around this idea of momentum from the indwelling presence of God, I would like to discuss three prophetic pictures from the Old Testament. Each one is full of prophetic power for the Christian in the twenty-first century. These are action images from the people of Israel that correlate to action steps for the people of God under the new covenant.

The three images are as follows: the seed of the woman, found in the Genesis Creation story; the seed of Abraham, connected to the Old Testament covenant; and the seed of David, connected to the emerging concept of the kingdom of God. All three connect to the idea of a spiritual seed with inherent promise for life. The seed is the potential for momentum to explode in the heart of those who respond by faith to God's Word.

Whenever God sees a problem, He looks for a remedy to resolve the problem. That remedy looks like a seed deposited in the heart or life of a man or woman of faith. These three are monumental seed stories from the Old Testament that will stretch our thinking so that we can think big and act big! All three seed stories release the momentum of holy action in our lives so that we can see God use our lives in ways beyond ourselves.

GO-BIG QUESTIONS

1. *Momentum* means "the force gained by a
    _____."

2. Small steps of _____, combined with prayer, surrender, and the Word, are the raw ingredients for a spiritual _____.

3. Momentum is our God-given cry for _____.

4. What ways are you called to invade, influence, and impact this generation? Share your thoughts below.

_____

_____

_____

THE SEED OF THE WOMAN: TRANSFORMATION FOR OUR FEET

E VERYONE KNOWS THE story: a garden, a cunning serpent, a piece of fruit, a tree, and the two main characters, Adam and Eve. It is a story of epic proportions because it affects the entirety of humanity. In one moment the destiny of mankind was hijacked by a diabolical plan. Sin was conceived, and with it, death. Trying to put this story into context for the modern reader is difficult, simply because of the massive implications it contains.

A proper understanding of the story and the subsequent consequences of disobedience are tragic. We see paradise compromised, humanity enslaved, death released, evil prevailing, and sin released into the human heart. It's all so fast paced that we can easily overlook the reach of the story into the twenty-first century. A quick overview will illustrate this well. Sickness? Stress? Sorrow? Death? Sin? Yes, it all goes back to the garden.

The enemy of humanity is really the enemy of God. Once forced out of heaven as the worship leader, he was bent on retaliation. Yet, he was unable to do so directly. So, he used a much more subtle means to vent his rebellious frustration. He used the image-bearers of the holy God, humanity, as his weapon to assault heaven. He comes to kill, steal, and destroy to lash out against the King because he knows that his time is short. It all sounds pretty horrific, and it is.

So is this story a colossal failure for the purposes of God? Is humanity doomed to subjugation to the tyranny of evil? Obviously, we know the answer is a resounding no. Jesus has come to redeem humanity, to heal the wound of the garden and restore our God-given identity. Yet, we often overlook the fact that the Cross was no haphazard strategy; it was strategic. The Cross was planned long before the whole mess unfolded. God had a plan for salvation and restoration. That plan was a seed.

We enter the garden narrative in Genesis 3 as the Creator is judging the sin of disobedience. In the development of this story we find the foundation for the old covenant and, ultimately, the new covenant too. God pronounces judgment on the serpent. In verse 15 the words are remarkable.

> And I will put enmity between you and the woman, and between your offspring and hers; he will crush your head, and you will strike his heel. (NIV)

Notice several key components of this extraordinary prophetic word released to Adam and Eve in the garden. There will be contention, resistance, and strife between humanity and the kingdom of darkness for perpetuity. Yet, all is not lost, because the redemptive plan of God includes a seed to be born to the woman and her lineage. This imagery is rich. Redemption is already in the workings for the evil of darkness to be completely negated.

The heel of the seed will be struck, indicating the sorrow and suffering of the Cross. It was at Calvary that Jesus's body was beaten and bloodied for the sin of all humanity. Yet, the seed will ultimately triumph. Jesus didn't stay in the grave. He rose from the dead. The promise is clear: He will crush the head of the serpent. Sin will not gain the upper hand in this struggle; Satan will not prevail.

As the Son of God, Jesus enters the story as the Son of Man to represent all of humanity, so that the sons of men—you and I—can recover our God-given identity as sons of God. As the seed of the woman, *Jesus represents all of humanity, so that His victory becomes our victory. Jesus is the triumph for every person!*

This is the image of our heart being redeemed, or bought back, from the tyranny of sin. By faith Christ releases His salvation into our heart. Part of this redemptive purpose has to do with our identity and authority. Once we recover these essential components, we are empowered to join with Jesus in the ultimate expression of His victory: reclaiming what rightfully belonged to humanity. *This is the imagery of feet being healed.* Satan, sickness, poverty—because of His ultimate victory, they are under our feet, even though sometimes our heart will tell us that they're not.

Our feet are created to go and to crush. These are two distinct aspects of the feet. The first correlates with the idea of mission. This missional aspect of our feet is beautifully depicted in Isaiah 52:7, where the prophet tells us, "How beautiful on the mountains are the feet of those who bring good news, who proclaim peace, who bring good tidings, who proclaim salvation, who say to Zion, 'Your God reigns!'" (NIV).

With our feet we bring good tidings that people are no longer in bondage to sin. Our feet are beautiful. Our feet have purpose. Our feet deliver the message of the good news: people no longer have to be enslaved to Satan. No wonder the devil lashes out at the heel of the seed. He wants to stop the message from reaching more hearts and changing more lives. Jesus comes to heal our feet so that we can participate in the glorious momentum of His redemptive purposes. *Sharing the good news of Jesus Christ is an act of warfare against the kingdom of darkness, and Satan knows it!*

For this reason, we experience backlash, resistance, hindrances, and assaults to prevent the message from reaching its destination. This is what many refer to as spiritual warfare. Satan knows the power of the gospel seed once planted in the heart! He fears it greatly, for it is has the potential for the person and image of Christ to be formed in another human life. He must try to stop this seed from being disseminated.

Fortunately, we are not powerless in this battle. The second aspect of our feet deals with this idea of authority. *Our feet have the power to crush Satan.* When it comes to the idea of crushing, many believers are really timid. After all, the slavery of sin has done a deep work to destroy our sense of confidence. Once in Christ, however, we recover our God-given mandate for authority.

What is our relationship to the devil now that we have been born again? Our feet are on top of him! Sometimes we see the enemy over us, infecting us, or possessing us. Let's also remember, though, that he sees us stomping him. We have more power in our feet than he does in all of the darkness. Jesus lives inside of us. *It is Christ in us, the hope of glory, that teaches our feet to trample the forces of the enemy as we continue walking by faith!*

The key idea here is that *we gain momentum as we crush the enemy's plans.* The seed planted in our life heals our heart, which in turn eventually heals our feet. We then begin to walk in real spiritual authority. Consider how this applies to the believer's thought patterns. Once we realize that our feet have been healed, we no longer think like victims; we realize that we are victors. The seed of the woman lives inside of us, giving us more and more confidence in this spiritual battle. We need to show the devil our feet. He's not over us. He's not in us. He's under us. Our thinking becomes faith-filled thinking, because we realize that we are serving on the winning side.

Christ within us as the hope of glory brings healing to our feet. Your feet have been healed! This isn't pretense; it's the reality of mission and authority in the life of a believer. When you walk into a room you are the seed to set the captive free. You now have the power to act big!

GO-BIG QUESTIONS

1. Jesus represents all of humanity so His victory becomes
   _____.

2. Sharing the _____ of Jesus Christ is an act of
   _____ against the kingdom of darkness.

3. Our feet have the power to _____.

4. How should we respond when we experience backlash, resistance, hindrances, and assaults? Share your thoughts below.

_____

_____

_____

DAY 15

THE SEED OF ABRAHAM: THE TRANSFORMATION OF OUR HANDS

ABRAHAM IS A very interesting Bible character. He is called to leave a place we have never heard of to go to a place he has never heard of. In fact, God doesn't even tell him where he is going when he first sets out on this journey of faith. Can you see the conversation unfolding with his polytheistic family members?

Abraham: "God, told me to leave Ur."

Family members: "God?"

Abraham: "Yes."

Family members: "Which God?"

Abraham: "The only God."

Family members: "There's only one God?"

Abraham: "Yes."

Family members: "And He spoke to you?"

Abraham: "Yes."

Family members: "And this God told you to do what?"

Abraham: "To leave here and go into the unknown."

Obviously, this story doesn't make any sense to the rational mind-set. From the perspective of faith, however, it makes total sense. God was asking Abraham to walk by total faith. This kind of walk demanded trust in God's sufficiency to lead, guide, and provide. A huge aspect of the provision and direction hinged on God's desire to bless Abraham.

God blessed Abraham in Genesis 12. *The blessing would involve a great name, a land, and nations.* Many people have taken these verses to teach prosperity for prosperity's sake;

however, I believe the blessing is not for selfish multiplication but rather to be a blessing to the nations of the world. God made a covenant with Abraham to ensure the promised blessing would be fulfilled. *Abraham's hands would be blessed to be a blessing to all the families of the earth.*

Part of the blessing was that God promised Abraham a seed to perpetuate this covenant of blessing. We often use the phrase "the seed of Abraham" from the reference to this idea in Galatians 3:16. Jesus Christ is the ultimate fulfillment of this promise. In that promise, Christ has come to heal our feet, but additionally, He has come to heal our hands as well. All in Christ Jesus are recipients of this blessing.

Our feet are for conquering the devil, but our hands are to be used for God and humanity. Paul tells us to lift "holy hands without anger or disputing" (1 Tim. 2:8, NIV). We are called to lay hands on the sick so that they can recover (Mark 16:18). Paul also tells us to be cautious "in the laying on of hands" (1 Tim. 5:22). Why? Simply because our hands have tremendous power for the Lord! They must be used to bless.

Yet, because of the curse we clench our hands into fists. People often justify the first because of their trials and problems. Our world is now a place full of fists. It's the mind-set that says, "Mess with me, and I'll hurt you." This is totally opposite of Jesus Christ and Abraham. *Jesus redeems us from the curse of the fist so that we can use our hands to bless God and men.* Sadly, many others have used their hands to assault the face of another human being. This is like slapping the glory of God or telling someone, "You don't have the glory God gave you."

The momentum we are talking about is getting delivered from an incorrect mind-set so that we see that our hands have power to serve and to bless. We are not here to hit with fists. *We are here to open our hands wide to be vessels of service to the world around us.* Our hands have the capacity to reach out and touch other people. The seed of Abraham, Jesus Christ, lives in our heart so that we can tell others, "I'm blessed to bless others with my hands."

We need a different kind of mind-set in how we see ourselves. Our hands have been healed! And they now have divine power.

Often we see everything in the Word of God from a spiritual dimension without realizing the physical dimension of the gospel. Acts tells us that God poured out His Spirit on all *flesh*, not on spirits. *The living reality of Christ within enables us to utilize our hands for His glory.* Let me illustrate with a story of what I mean.

In 1991 I was preaching in Michigan for a series of meetings. A couple who were connected to Haiti came to hear me speak. They invited the Haitian pastor they supported to attend the meetings. He objected because I am a Pentecostal. This brother considered Pentecostalism just as strange as voodoo. Through much coercion this brother finally agreed to attend. He sat in the meetings, but he was not happy. I found out that he was the leader of an entire organization in Haiti and pastored two hundred of the most intelligent people in the country.

He came to hear me a second time. On the third day I sensed the Lord wanted to break through in his life, so I fasted to preach to one person. I felt prompted that evening to challenge everyone by saying, "If you love God, stand up, and if you don't, stay where you are." Obviously, no one wanted to deny the love of Jesus, so everyone responded to this invitation. I followed this up with, "If you want more of God, come forward, and if you don't, stay where you are."

The pastor came up to the front with everyone else, so I prayed for him. As I kept walking past him, I decided to look back behind me. This dear brother was under the front row seats. He stayed in a heavenly trance with no food or water for two days. The following Monday I went to his house to pray for him. He revived and said that he had been in the presence of God for three days. Christ in me, the hope of glory, had used my hands as a connection point for transformation in this brother's life.

More than twenty-one years later I decided to contact this brother. I had never been to Haiti and had no interaction with him since Michigan. I wanted to go to Haiti to see what God had done in his life. He wanted me to come preach at his church, but I just wanted to visit with him. We finally reached a compromise that I would share for a few minutes with his prayer group that met on Wednesday afternoons before returning to the United States.

Much to my surprise there were seven thousand people in attendance for the prayer meeting in the middle of the afternoon! A voodoo priest was in attendance and started manifesting demons during the meeting. Another woman was involved in satanic rituals and also started manifesting. Both were immediately surrounded by the believers in attendance, and as they laid hands on them and prayed the devils were cast out.

God had done an incredible work in this brother's life! As I left this dear brother told me that if I would come back on a weekend I could speak to his congregation of some twenty thousand–plus people.

Our hands were made to bless! Our hands were made to heal. Our hands are lethal weapons in God's kingdom. *We now have the power to act big because our hands are healed.*

Go-Big Questions

1. Our feet are for conquering the _____, but our hands are for _____ and _____.

2. Jesus redeems us from the _____ of the fist so that we can use our _____ to bless God and men.

3. Our hands are lethal _____ in God's kingdom.

4. In what ways can you use your hands to bless others? Share your thoughts below.

_____

_____

_____

THE SEED OF DAVID: TRANSFORMATION FOR OUR HEART

D avid is one of the most beloved characters in the Old Testament. He possesses a certain measure of underdog allure that draws the reader into the account. As a youth he singlehandedly defeats the giant. He then becomes one of the leading generals in the nation of Israel. His popularity soars so high that even King Saul is overshadowed. The story is full of modern intrigue: promotion, jealousy, suspicion, and injustice.

On the run from a crazy king, David resorted to hiding in caves and feigning insanity. Yet, his exploits in leading his band of rogues are legendary. His character was impeccable. And his passion for God was extraordinary. Reading the Psalms is a rare glimpse into the heart of a God-hungry leader. His transparency appeals to a wide audience of disappointed and wounded readers. His relationship with God was nothing short of authentic. Yes, David is quite the character: spiritually vibrant, militarily unstoppable, politically savvy, and domestically challenged.

He had the heart of a leader, the heart of a worshiper, as well as the heart of a champion. If there is one idea that summarizes the life of David it is the phrase *heart after God.* In fact, the New Testament references David's heart for God in the Book of Acts as his strongest characteristic. God spoke of him through the Holy Spirit centuries after his death.

> After removing Saul, he made David their king. God testified concerning him: "I have found David son of Jesse, a man after my own heart; he will do everything I want him to do."
>
> —ACTS 13:22

The lesson is powerful. God moved in David's life based on the condition of his heart. David had a heart after God's own heart. For this reason God knew David would be capable of accomplishing God's purpose in his generation.

David's life is characterized by a defining moment when God makes a covenant with him concerning his seed. We find the story in 2 Samuel, chapter 7. David sensed a strong desire to build a house for God. That night God appeared to Nathan and told him that David wasn't the man for the job due to the blood David had shed! Nevertheless, the Lord made a glorious promise to David. It was a covenant to him and his family.

> When your days are over and you rest with your ancestors, I will raise up your offspring to succeed you, your own flesh and blood, and I will establish his kingdom. He is the one who will build a house for my Name, and I will establish the throne of his kingdom forever.
>
> —2 SAMUEL 7:12–13, NIV

The covenant promise made to David in this verse finds immediate fulfillment in the life of Solomon. Yet, it is much bigger than the next king of Israel. It is a prophetic picture of the Messiah, the Lord Jesus Christ, establishing the kingdom of God. The seed of David would blossom into the full reign of God in the hearts of men.

What was the purpose of this kingdom and this promised King? It was to heal the human heart. Just as David was a man after God's own heart, so through Jesus Christ everyone who responds to His simple message by faith can have their heart transformed.

What is the essence of this heart of David? I think it was his willingness to surrender his time to be with God. David was a man who prized intimacy with God above everything else. He touched the very heart of God by his hunger for a personal relationship with God. The more he immersed himself in God's presence, the more God blessed his life. The more his heart hungered for the holy, the more the Holy released an image of the kingdom through David's life. We are given a glimpse of the glories of the kingdom through the heart of David.

I want to inspire your faith that the kingdom of God can be manifested around you. I believe this happens as we respond to the invitation of heaven: "Come away from everything else and seek My face." As we do this with the same hungry, Davidic heart for intimacy we are enabled to demonstrate God's power and authority. The kingdom is manifested through our lives. It all starts with the heart. Jesus told us, "Where your treasure is, there your heart will be also" (Luke 12:34). *The heart of intimacy is a surrendered heart.* It is a heart invested in the kingdom of God. The more we surrender our heart in this place of communion, the more our heart is healed and conformed to the glory of Christ.

The power of Christ is inside of us. Let me ask a question: What was nailed to the cross? The nails stopped His hands and His feet from letting His body fall, but they didn't kill him. It was our sin that held Christ to the cross. Jesus didn't die from the stripes on His back or from the crown of thorns. He died from a broken heart. He was willing to allow the wrath of God to punish Him so that our hearts could be healed. This is glorious imagery of the seed of David. Jesus heals our heart! He comes to transform the world around us by releasing the glory of His kingdom through us.

Our hearts have incredible significance in the kingdom of God; they are the domains of the kingdom. The kingdom atmosphere of eternity and glory can come in the midst of time to touch us at the deepest parts of our heart. It is here that our attitudes and motivations intersect with the eternal kingdom.

The work of the Spirit of God is to reveal to us that our attitude is as important as our actions. As I have already alluded to earlier in this book, whatever gets our attention gets us. Whatever has our thoughts owns us.

We are so conditioned to evaluate from an external, action-based perspective. We think that people who do certain things are bad and are going to hell. Yet, we overlook the secret realities of the heart. This issue of the heart is exactly what Christ confronted in His Sermon on the Mount. Jesus shows us that a spirit of gossip is essentially the same thing as the spirit of murder, except it's done with a tongue instead of a bullet.

The idea is that the surrender of our heart must always involve our attitude and actions. Only then can we truly experience the heart of David. The intimacy of God's presence transforms us! Paul's revelation that Christ living in us is the hope of glory becomes a reality. We must experience the Lord's power and presence in this generation! Manifestation of the kingdom is connected to our heart. We need intimacy! We need the heart of David.

It is time to act big, kingdom big! Let's allow our hearts to manifest His presence so the kingdom of God can be experienced in and through our lives. Only His presence can bring the transformation our world needs.

GO-BIG QUESTIONS

1. David had the heart of a _____, the heart of a _____, as well as the heart of a _____.

2. The purpose of _____ is to heal the human heart.

3. The _____ is a surrendered heart.

4. What does it mean to have a heart of intimacy? Share your thoughts below.

_____

_____

_____

TRANSFORMATION IN VERTICAL RELATIONSHIP

WE HAVE LOOKED at the three seeds of covenant in the Old Testament and how they connect to the New Testament covenant. Through the Cross of Christ we have been transformed. Our capacity for kingdom action has been restored. This is described through the images we have examined together: transformation for the feet, transformation for the hands, and transformation of the heart. We are now empowered to act big for God's glory.

How does this powerful transformation now affect our lives? What does transformation look like in terms of *acting big*? The first area that we want to discuss is our relationship with God. This is the vertical component of transformation. It is a highly relational component of what it means to be a believer. It is grounded in the love of God! His love grounds us and anchors to covenant. From this place we enter into relationship.

Many people who have a relationship with Christ understand their walk with Christ in relational terms. We have been born again. We are now sons and daughters. We have been brought into the family of the glorious Father. The deposit of His Spirit connects us to this glorious lineage. Heaven is our final destination. We have promises of glory and eternal pleasures. The inheritance is magnificent yet very much unseen except by the eyes of faith. In other words, it's more real than the air we breathe but just as elusive as the air as well.

We would be inclined to assume that a member of a vibrant, dynamic family with incredible promise would have tremendous relational connections with the other members. Yet, the average Christian talks about their walk with the Lord mostly in the past tense: "I was born again." "I accepted Christ." "I heard His voice." "He spoke to me." "He touched my heart." "He worked powerfully in my life."

Obviously, the past tense is powerful because it connects history to our testimony. Recalling God's past faithfulness gives us courage to believe Him for the future. The effect is similar on other believers who hear our experiences. I am a great advocate of recounting God's faithfulness in the past. Yet, it's all too easy to become so absorbed by events and experiences that will never happen again that we miss the present. And this is where many believers get trapped. They hope for a vision. They celebrate the past but make no correlation in the present to connect the two. God is a God of the present just as much as the past and the future.

The challenge is a relational one. *Present-tense testimonies and moves of God only happen when we are present in our relationship with Him in the here and now.* Does God have great things planned for our life in the future? Surely He does! Yet, we must never forget that the present is the door to that future. Our present relationship with Jesus ensures our future experience of His goodness.

My experience shows me that many believers aren't really connected to the present though. Their thinking is contaminated with problems and challenges that inadvertently minimize God's power and glory in their current situations. Many people struggle in connecting the challenges of today with the God of this moment. Somehow, the relational component is compromised. Let me be clear. I don't mean this indicates a breach in relationship. We are born-again, and we love the Lord. Yet, too often a disconnect takes place when we begin to talk about our personal, ongoing relational experience with the Lord.

One easy example to grasp is our prayer life. Following the same vein of thought about a dynamic family, wouldn't it make sense to say that a member of that family would long to spend a concerted time immersed in other family members' presence? I love my son, Jon; his wife, Dori; and my grandchildren, Sophie, J, and Caden. Every chance I get my wife, Marsha, and I make arrangements to connect with them. We love being around each other. We love hanging out, laughing, telling stories, and sharing memories.

If we take this image to our relationship with our heavenly family, we would expect the same kind of intimacy. Sadly, most believers don't discuss their relationship with God in these terms. They view Him as somehow removed and distant. Or maybe He is angry, uninterested, just too busy. I think you get the idea.

The other aspect of the disconnect takes place in the image of ourselves. We see ourselves as unworthy, disqualified, too anxious, fearful, etc. When these two broken images are put together, this broken image of how we see God as well as the broken image of how we see ourselves lead to a struggle in the now. Our present relationship with God will be challenged.

The three images from the Old Testament that we have seen so far are a key to restoring this relational dynamic. We have healed feet. We have healed hands. We have a healed heart. These are realities that Christ has already accomplished for us by His Cross.

Our feet have authority not only to crush the devil but also to stand in the holy place to commune with the Father. Our hands have been healed not only to bless and to minister life to other people but also to bless the Lord in worship! Our heart has been healed to experience the intimacy that David knew in His walk with the Lord. We have been gifted with a glorious capacity to know and be known by the same covenant-keeping God as David knew. This will revolutionize our experience with God in the present. We will hear His voice with much more clarity and confidence. Our lives will be marked by a sense of purpose and direction. Intimacy and presence will characterize our heart's experience.

Hopefully you have already started to feel the impact of these truths in your life. Unfortunately, old habits and, especially, old thinking patterns are not easy to change. They are embedded deep in our minds. New information comes along that contradicts the old patterns of thinking, and we are suddenly faced with an internal dilemma. Will we hold on to the old? It's comfortable to think the way that we always have. We have even developed certain assumptions about God and about ourselves based on this old pattern of thinking.

Do we drop the old and cling to the new? Do we embrace the reality of transformation? If it stays as a nice idea in a book it probably will have no means of transforming our thoughts and intersecting with our current relationship with God. This is why I love to ask people when I preach about this subject to start talking to themselves. Some people are very reserved at first. I tell them, "Say to your hands, 'Be healed.' Tell your feet, 'Feet, you are healed.' Tell your heart, 'Heart, you are new.'" Maybe it does sound crazy, but I can tell you that there is power in affirming these realities. It greatly helps us begin to change the pattern of our thinking!

This is where we have to make a choice. If we are going to think like Jesus, then we are going to have break with old patterns and embrace truth. This is action. This is present tense. This is now. We need our thoughts revamped so that we can act big in this generation! We have been invited into this glorious relationship of freedom. Let's not squander it.

Go-Big Questions

1. The past tense can be very powerful because it connects _____ to our _____.

2. Present-tense testimonies and moves of God only happen when we are _____ in our relationship with Him in the here and now.

3. In order to develop our relationship with God we need to focus on our _____.

4. What ways in your life can you act big for God? Share your thoughts below.

_____

_____

_____

DAY 18
TRANSFORMATION IN HORIZONTAL RELATIONSHIPS

THE SECOND AREA of transformation that we are going to look at in this book is the horizontal dynamic of relationship. Our growing understanding of Christ in us being the hope of glory must find expression in our relationships with people around us.

When the expert in the Law confronted Jesus with a question of priority in the Word of God, Jesus offered two answers. The first and most important thing is to "love the Lord...with all your heart...with all your soul and with all your mind" (Matt. 22:37). We see here a picture of what we discussed in the previous chapter. We see a vibrant vertical relationship involving surrender and dedication. The word *all* indicates that love involves every aspect of our being.

As we respond to His love we find more and more of us opening up in full surrender to the glory of knowing Jesus. Again, this is the vertical side of transformation. We respond to His love by offering all of our heart! Sounds like David and His intimacy. We respond to His love by surrendering our mind. This is the very essence of this book: *thinking like Jesus.* He is transforming us for His glory.

Jesus continued with the second priority. He told the expert of the Law representing the religious system of that day that he needed to love his neighbor as himself. Most know the next part of the passage. Jesus told a parable about the good Samaritan. The concept has become integrated into our culture. When someone goes over and beyond what is expected of them in service of another, even giving of themselves sacrificially, then they are deemed a good Samaritan. It's easy to get so caught up with the parable Jesus tells, full of vivid imagery and cultural intrigue, that we miss the correlation between the first priority Jesus stated and the second. There is a very real connection between the vertical and the horizontal.

Jesus made it abundantly clear that we are to love our neighbors as we love ourselves. This is where the horizontal capacity for action often breaks down in the lives of many believers. We see the wounded, the destitute, the suffering, and the broken, yet our sense of compassion is hardly stirred. We have no heart for our neighbors. We have no desire to reach out to the wounded and weary traveler on the highway of life. And we certainly aren't about to sacrificially give of our time and resources to nurse them back to health. What is the issue? How can we be so orthodox in our profession of Christianity and yet so slow in our willingness to turn into action?

Could it be that we have no love for ourselves? Many people recoil at the thought. "Love for myself? Sounds like some kind of pagan notion for self-indulgence." Yet, Jesus is very clear in His explanation to the religious of His day. Love for self precedes love for the neighbor. And love for God precedes love for self. It seems like a kingdom pattern for transformation.

Here is the pattern I see. God loves us. We respond to that love by loving Him back. The more we love, the more we experience inner healing and restoration. This produces confidence to love ourselves. We recognize the personal expression of Jesus in our lives. This confidence produces motivation to love others.

The good Samaritan in this story must have really loved himself deeply to be able to give of himself so extravagantly! Ultimately, this is what we see in the greatest good Samaritan of all, Jesus Christ. His was a perfect sacrifice because He knew the love of God perfectly.

Yet, here is the main challenge. Many believers really don't love themselves. In fact, if they were honest, they can barely stand themselves. Many are covered with shame, bound with self-hatred, and shackled by rejection. They are so self-focused that there is no room for horizontal relationships. Simply stated, they have never learned to love themselves.

Such people will never be effective in loving others.

This is tragic. *The connection point between Christ living in our hearts and Christ encountering other people is us.* It's just plain old you and me. We are Jesus's hands and feet. The deposit of His glory in our lives is designed to touch other people. It is designated for that purpose. Let me give a quick illustration of this to make it more practical.

Often my ministry receives designated funds. We are responsible and accountable to the particular donor for directing those resources as they intended. I am not free to use them at my own discretion. The same is true of the Spirit of Christ in the believer. The Spirit of Christ is deposited into our lives and designated to be used according to heaven's purpose. Often I find that many believers don't realize that they are stewards. We understand this in terms of finances, but we are also stewards of the deposit of Christ inside our lives. Sadly, it is possible to be hindered from discharging this trust because our lives are so broken.

Jesus comes to restore our heart. He heals our hands. He transforms our feet, not for us alone but so that we can be healed for service. As we are transformed internally we find freedom for external service. In fact, the work of the Spirit is so liberating that we find our heart compelled to reach out to others. We desire them to experience the same healing that we have known. We desire their lives to know the same depth of Christ's love that we have tasted. Action always follows holy motivation. The effect of the kingdom of God in our heart is released through us to impact others.

This is horizontal transformation. Our thinking becomes outward focused instead of self-absorbed. Our focus and attitude shift from our own pain to others' pain. As our heart is healed we find holy action stirring us to reach out of comfort zones. Other people begin to experience the reality of the kingdom. They are set free. God is glorified, and we get to be a part of heaven's purposes in others' lives.

Act big! God will be glorified, and people will be impacted.

GO-BIG QUESTIONS

1. When we grow in our understanding of Christ in us being the hope of glory we must find _____ in our _____ with people around us.

2. As we respond to God's love we find more and more of us opening up in full _____ to the _____ of knowing Jesus.

3. The connection point between Christ living in our _____ and Christ encountering other people is _____.

4. In what ways can you share God's love with others every day? Share your thoughts below.

_____

_____

_____

TRANSFORMATION IN INTERNAL RELATIONSHIP

THE THIRD AREA of transformation that we need to explore is the idea of the internal relationship. This is where we touch on identity. *Christ inside of a believer alters our concept of God, others, and ultimately, ourselves.* Truth be told, this is probably the most difficult of the three areas for most people to embrace. It is entirely possible to view God from a new relational paradigm and see the implications of this reality of service toward those around us and yet miss the implications of personal identity. Many believers are still trapped by the snare of shame and the shackles of rejection. This is so tragic!

The most important thing in life next to peace with God is peace with oneself. Without it, life is absolutely miserable. Relationships are damaged, and our kingdom purpose is squandered.

The gospel message is an inclusive message. Many believers understand that the gospel has to do with redemption of the soul so that we can experience eternal life. This is powerful. Our soul needs to be redeemed. Yet, this is never the end goal of the Christian faith. If it were, Jesus would save us and then immediately promote us to heaven. Christ in us as the hope of glory involves the ongoing redemptive work of Christ to save our whole being. This speaks of emotional, psychological, and physical aspects of our entity. Jesus is after the whole person.

When it comes to this idea of identity we are talking about self-perception. How do we see ourselves? What do we think about ourselves? How has the life of Christ transformed how we view ourselves? The answer to these questions determines what we believe about ourselves. Beliefs are powerful because they influence action.

The answer to these questions also reveals what we identify with in life. We all love to belong somewhere and with someone. Where we belong touches the idea of identity. It is shaped in large part by what we believe. In other words, even if we believe God wants to be involved in the present (see day 17 of this devotional), and even if we have faith to serve others around us (see day 18), our identity will remain affected if we continue to view ourselves negatively. We will make little kingdom impact.

As our beliefs are transformed, so must our identity be transformed, shaping us into the person that Christ can use to accomplish kingdom action. This is so critical. These three areas of transformation in vertical, horizontal, and internal paradigms must line up with the reality of Christ in us in order for the kingdom of God to become tangible in our lives.

I like to talk about this idea when I'm speaking by using three B words: *believe, belong,* and *become.* What we believe affects where we belong and ultimately what we become. Christ inside of us is the deposit from heaven to guarantee that we become who Christ is calling us to be. This entire process is based on surety of God's love. He loves us too much to leave us the way He first encountered us. He is committed to the ongoing process of helping us be whole.

For many, our thoughts and our beliefs are on two different planes. We say we believe the central truths of the Word of God, but when we analyze our thought patterns we find negativity, fear, rejection, shame, isolation, and anger controlling our behaviors. Why is this? I believe the answer is because our identity in Christ is not whole. We are fragmented.

The result is that we back down from what God has called us to. Our kingdom action is inhibited and often completely thwarted. We rationalize our disobedience with many different excuses. However, the primary issue remains the same: our identity is fragmented, so we lack the inner fortitude to take the risk of obedience.

Fragmentation is the idea that we are broken into multiple pieces. Here's an example: The spiritual part of our existence receives eternal life through faith in Christ when we are born again. We sense wholeness in this area. Yet, in relational terms we have wounds from past experiences. This causes us to view ourselves through the lens of rejection. The end result is that we are sure of our salvation but very intimidated to open up our heart to anyone, including God. This is fragmentation—two pieces of the whole broken apart and lacking cohesion and consistency.

Jesus comes to restore our broken heart to wholeness. When we are fragmented it is very easy to move into a place of unintentional hypocrisy. Our actions contradict what we believe because our heart is wounded. Our perception of ourselves is tainted, so we flounder spiritually.

Consider the image of a very wealthy investor making his greatest investment. Where would we expect him to place it? In a bank? A vault? A protected safety deposit box? Deposits of great worth are only made in places of extreme confidence and value.

Jesus deposits His glory in our hearts! The value He places on the redeemed human heart can't be overestimated. The treasure of heaven has been placed inside our broken lives as a seed. This seed of glory now has the potential to release glory. I've found that the best remedy for fragmentation is glory. His weighty presence brings healing into our inner being. He sets us free from the lies and perceptions that have shackled us by giving us truth.

This is how He demonstrates His ongoing love for us. He keeps releasing more glory to heal our fragmented hearts. Rejection is drowned by the assurance of His glorious love. Fear is cast out by this same love. Shame is smashed by His love. This is a mystery—the God of heaven and Earth revealing His Son inside of us. The broken places come into contact with Christ's brokenness, and the end result is healing. The broken pieces of our identity are unified to produce a beautiful new sense of wholeness.

Whole people are people of action. They have no hesitation in the face of the enemy's jeers. They don't back down from others people's taunts. They are free to act! Vertically, they pursue intimacy with God. Horizontally, they are effective in their pursuit of service to mankind. And internally, their identity is whole to pursue purpose. Christ in us as the hope of glory makes all the difference in the world.

Think big—believe! Act big—believe.

GO-BIG QUESTIONS

1. Christ inside of a believer alters our concept of
   _____, others, and _____.

2. The most important thing in life next to _____
   with God is peace with _____.

3. _____ is the idea that we are broken into
   _____ pieces.

4. How can you match God's thoughts to yours about what
   He thinks of you? Share your thoughts below.

   _____

   _____

   _____

DAY 20
TRANSFORMATION IN THINKING

JESUS LOVES TO heal the places of fragmentation in our lives so we can be whole. Whole people are Jesus thinkers. They are able to view themselves positively, see others in a healthy light, and interact with God in a life-giving present reality. When these three paradigms are whole, we can think God's thoughts freely.

Years ago I heard someone say that the most important gift they could give anyone is peace of mind. Freedom from anxiety, stress, and confusion is a great asset in anyone's life. Yet, I believe Jesus takes it one step further. Not only is He the author of peace in our minds, but He is the author of peaceful attitudes. Thoughts form attitudes. Attitudes direct decisions of the will. The will determines our actions. And ultimately, our actions form our consequences or rewards.

I've alluded to this idea already in this book. It is good to reiterate it here so that we can again be reminded of the importance of our thinking. Probably Chuck Swindoll writes the best insight on attitude that I've ever found. It is a poem that articulates the power of attitude:

> Attitude, to me, is more important than education, than money, than circumstances, than failures, than successes, than what other people think or say or do. It is more important than appearance, giftedness or skill. It will make or break a company...a church...a home. The remarkable thing is we have a choice every day regarding the attitude we embrace for that day. We cannot change our past...we cannot change the fact that people act in a certain way. We cannot change the inevitable. The only thing we can do is play on the one string we have, and that is our attitude...I am convinced that life is 10 percent what happens to me and 90 percent how I react to it. And so it is with you...We are in charge of our attitudes.[1]

Attitude is powerful stuff!

Jesus wants us to think like He thinks. One of the major aspects of this is attitude. The dictionary defines *attitude* as "a settled way of thinking or feeling about someone or something, typically one that is reflected in a person's behavior."[2] We see Jesus's attitude clearly detailed in Philippians chapter 2. The New Living Translation of verse 5 reads this way, "You must have the same attitude that Christ Jesus had." The King James Version tells us, "Let this same mind be in you, which was also in Christ Jesus."

So what was Christ's attitude? What mind-set did He have that we need to implement? The following verses unpack this idea for us.

Jesus didn't take equality with God as something to be clung to. This would have been so easy and so right! Jesus was God; why not act like God? Why not receive worship as God? Instead, He gave up His divine privileges and took the position of a slave. He appeared in human form and humbled Himself in obedience to God by dying a criminal's death on the cross. The result of His decision was that every knee will bow and every tongue confess that Jesus Christ is Lord.

So what is the attitude of Christ? Humility: Jesus opted for an attitude of humility. Submission: He embraced a mind-set of submission to the Father. Suffering: Suffering for righteousness' sake was embraced. The will of God was elevated. His pride and prestige were sacrificed for slavery to the will of God. Self-preservation was executed for the sake of humanity's redemption. What an attitude! What a challenge! What a calling for us to embrace!

So we can summarize this passage by saying that Jesus's attitude led to specific action steps. His manner of thinking affected His life, as well as countless others. *His attitude set the course for kingdom action.* God responded to such an attitude by releasing salvation to the human race in the exaltation of His Son.

Can you see the power of Jesus thinking? Thinking like Jesus by embracing His attitude will always produce salvation and breakthrough in lives around us! We are modeling Christ to others. When they grasp what is taking place they too will bow their knees and confess with their tongue that Jesus is the Lord.

Thinking like Jesus is really all about embracing a kingdom attitude. It is a willingness to surrender our plan and desires to the Father's. It is relinquishing our rights to become nothing. It is even openness to suffering for God's glory. These three alone are the exact opposite of what our culture teaches us. We are supposed to be self-asserting, entitled, and demanding. Jesus turns this upside down! His was no individual quest for preeminence. Rather, He was after the redemption of humanity. And so He had to think differently. He needed a kingdom mind-set, not a cultural one.

Jesus thinks big. He acts big. And He calls us to think big as well as to act big!

GO-BIG QUESTIONS

1. Jesus wants us to _____ like He _____.

2. The attitude of Christ is _____.

3. Embracing a kingdom _____ is a willingness to surrender our plan and desires to the Father's.

4. What steps do you need to take to obtain a kingdom attitude in your life? Share your thoughts below.

_____

_____

_____

TRANSFORMATION OF LOVE

THE THREE PARADIGMS that we have examined in the past three chapters revolve around the most critical aspect of the gospel: love. Christ in us, the hope of glory, is based on the surety of God's love expressed in our lives. Love is the most powerful human emotion. We all yearn for it. We cannot live without it. And yet it is so expansive, so all-encompassing, that there is no way to measure it, prove it, define it, or even describe it.

When we speak of the intellect, it is represented by the mind. In discussing the emotions, more specifically, the emotion of love, it is represented by the heart.

The symbol of the heart is one of the most well known in our modern era. It crosses continents, cultures, religions, and languages. The symbol of the little red heart means love. We use it to sign letters, to replace the word love, and we plaster it on cards, T-shirts, necklaces, balloons, and just about anything else we can mention.

How is the image of the heart, as we most know it, the symbol for this passionate experience of love? This is a really interesting question. I've found that the Hebrew month of Elul is the key to unlocking the connection between love and the heart. The Hebrew calendar contains twelve lunar months. Elul is the sixth month, corresponding with the months of August–September on our calendar. Interestingly, the Hebrew letters that form the word Elul, aleph, lamed, vav, and lamed, are an acronym in classical Hebrew thought for the expression found in the Song of Solomon, "ani l'dodi v'dodi li."[1] It means, "I am to my beloved and my beloved is to me."

This beautifully romantic phrase is an Old Testament picture of passionate love. It foreshadows our relationship with Christ, often paralleled to that of a husband and wife. The church is the bride, and Christ the groom.

One scholar writes this beautiful

> [Jewish commentary on the Torah, known as] the
> Zohar explains that at the beginning of the month
> of Elul humanity is *achor el achor,* meaning "Back
> to back," and by the end of Elul we are *panim el
> panim* meaning "face to face" [with God]. Yet how
> can it be that we are back to back [with God]?
> Wouldn't that imply that He has His back turned to
> us as well?[2]

Jewish commentary also teaches us that during Elul "the
King is in the field." If this is so, then this would be "the month
when God is most accessible."[3] He is waiting for us to run to
Him in the "field" of our everyday lives. So how do we make
sense of it?

The phrases *back to back* and *face to face* offer a powerful
object lesson. *Often, when we feel wounded, abandoned, hurt,
or whatever the root of our pain, we turn our back.* In doing this,
we have no idea of the other person's state. In this condition it
is easier to believe that we are not the only one with a turned
back. We like to imagine that the other person has also turned
around and refused to face us. If this is the case, then why
bother to turn around at all? Why make that first move, only to
turn around and see the back of the person we love?

This mental game, however, is the cause of many unresolved
arguments, wounded hearts, and damaged relationships. It
is an all too familiar scene from many romance movies. The
couple walks away from each other. At some point the man
turns around; he wants to call her name, ask for a second
chance, or plead for forgiveness. Just as he is about to speak he
realizes that her back is turned. She continues walking away.
He rationalizes that it is too late; her heart has grown cold. So
he turns his back.

Moments later, she turns to look at him. She yearns for the
relationship to continue. She wants to speak but can't find
the words. She lacks the courage, especially when she realizes
that his back is turned. She stares at him with longing, but it
seems pointless. She assumes he doesn't feel anything as he

continues to walk away from her. As viewers we sit on the edge of our seats, hoping that maybe they will both turn around simultaneously to finally realize that they both care, that neither wants to be back to back. They really desire to be face to face. Frequently this fairytale ending happens; sometimes it doesn't.

The month of Elul isn't teaching us that God's back is turned toward us at any particular moment of our lives. Rather, it is showing us the necessity of being willing to turn around. The King is in the field. Christ, the hope of glory, is in our heart, and no matter how we may feel, He has never had His back turned. He eagerly yearns for us to turn around and realize that He desires intimacy with us. The "back to back" notion that we experience at the beginning of the month is based on our misperceptions, our fears, and faulty presumptions.

Only when we turn around do we realize the truth: we are face to face, which not only means that we can look *at* each other but, more so, that we can experience the satisfying intimacy of being fully loved, fully embraced, and fully accepted by Christ's powerful love. *His love transforms us.*

It is entirely possible to walk in and out of power and remain the same. When we walk into His love, demonstrated by His blood spilled on the cross, we are changed.

It is this face-to-face encounter that transforms us: our perception of how we see ourselves, our perception of God, and our perception of others. It is here that Jesus meets us. His love removes the barrier of self-imposed isolation created by shame, fear, doubt, feelings of unworthiness, etc. As we encounter this powerful love we realize that His back was never turned in the first place.

We are loved. We are valued. We are chosen. Our heart can be delivered from the inner tirade of deception that keeps us removed from the hope of His glory. *Our heart can be free to think His thoughts!* His perfect love casts out our fear of failure, our fear of rejection, our fear of death, and every other fear that can be named (1 John 4:18). This is the foundation of being able to think big! We have encountered intimacy with

Jesus, the biggest thinker of them all. By His love we are able to think like He does!

GO-BIG QUESTIONS

1. Often, when we feel _____, abandoned, _____, or whatever the root of our pain, we turn our back.

2. God's love _____ us.

3. Our heart can be free to think Christ's _____!

4. How do you show God your love? Share your thoughts below.

_____

_____

_____

DAY 22
THE CHALLENGE OF TRANSFORMATION

Transformation is never an easy process. It requires great patience as well as great determination on our part to cooperate with God in the process.

We have explored many different facets of what this transformational process entails—the vertical dimension, the horizontal dimension, as well as the internal dimension. Christ's glorious presence living inside of our heart gives us the courage to keep turning toward God for the face-to-face intimacy that our soul desires. As we stay in His presence He accomplishes His ultimate purpose: transforming us to be like Jesus.

Paul states this purpose this way: "For those God foreknew he also predestined to be conformed to the image of his Son, that he might be the firstborn among many brothers and sisters" (Rom. 8:29).

Here is the glorious truth of this entire book. We are called to be like Jesus on this side of eternity! The purpose of being transformed isn't just for a better relationship with God or more active kingdom service toward others or even a better peace with ourselves. All of these are wonderful benefits of the ultimate purpose of the kingdom. We are called to be sons and daughters conformed to the image of Christ Jesus.

This is very weighty stuff. Christ's glory abiding inside of us is a transformational glory. The more we embrace His presence, the more we become like Jesus. The call of heaven in this hour is for family expansion. Jesus is the firstborn among many brothers and sisters.

I believe Romans 8:29 is talking about more than the positional transformation of salvation. Yes, we are sons and daughters because we have been born again. This truth can never be taken lightly. It is monumental. Yet, the application of this truth is what we are exploring in this entire book. Being born again is just the first step in the process of transformation; this verse is discussing the end goal of transformation.

What is that goal? *Ultimately, Jesus is looking for representation on the face of our planet.* He is seeking brothers and sisters who will manifest His character as well as demonstrate His power. The hour for a weak, wishy-washy church has passed. The argument of cheap grace, where we justify our carnality lightly, is no longer valid. The world is looking for something authentic, something genuine, something worthy of the name of Christ. They want to know if our experience in Jesus is legitimate. Otherwise, there is very little difference between our belief systems and the many other systems embraced on this earth.

This is challenging. Actually, this is incredibly challenging. It is not a task to be taken lightly to represent Christ.

Paul is the classic example of a follower of Christ who understood the goal of transformation and committed himself to manifesting Christlikeness. One of his primary approaches to discipleship was imitation. He not only shared powerful ideas in his letters, but he shared a transformed lifestyle with the churches. Let's look at a few examples.

> What you have learned and received and heard and seen *in me*—practice these things, and the God of peace will be with you.
> —PHILIPPIANS 4:9, EMPHASIS ADDED

Paul wants believers to practice the things they see in his life. In writing to Timothy, his spiritual son, he follows the same line of thought:

> You, however, have followed *my teaching, my conduct, my aim in life, my faith, my patience, my love, my steadfastness, my persecutions and sufferings* that happened to me at Antioch, at Iconium, and at Lystra.
> —2 TIMOTHY 3:10–11, EMPHASIS ADDED

He tells the carnal, stricken Christians of Corinth the same thing: "Be imitators of me, as I am of Christ" (1 Cor. 11:1). Again a few chapters earlier he states:

For though you have countless guides in Christ,
you do not have many fathers. For I became your
father in Christ Jesus through the gospel. *I urge
you, then, be imitators of me.* That is why I sent you
Timothy, my beloved and faithful child in the Lord,
to remind you of my ways in Christ, as I teach them
everywhere in every church.

—1 CORINTHIANS 4:15–17, EMPHASIS ADDED

To the church in Thessalonica it's the same story: "For you
yourselves know how *you ought to imitate us*" (2 Thess. 3:7,
emphasis added).

Are we able to tell those around us to copy what we do? Can
we encourage them to embrace our prayer life and implement
our devotional patterns? Would we ask them to think the
consistent thoughts in our minds? Would we be comfortable
to have them implement our relational dynamics in their
relationships? Could we tell them to use the same figures of
speech that we do in their conversations?

I could keep going, but I think the point has been made.
*In order to accurately represent Christ through discipleship in
people's lives there must be transformation in us.* How different
this sounds from the modern approach of spiritual leaders who
tell us to do what they say but not what they do. This model has
led to the spiritual demise of multitudes that label Christians
as hypocrites.

The principle is clear: Jesus calls us to be transformed and
represent Him well. Sin doesn't cause us to lose our position as
sons and daughters, but it sure does compromise our stature
and testimony before a wicked world. As we close this section
of this book I want to challenge us, including myself, with the
simple reminder that we are called to represent Christ.

Is this perfectionism and legalism all over again? Hardly.
This is *Christ transforming us from the inside out so that we can
conform to His image of holiness in our generation.* This is His
work by the power of His Spirit operating inside of us, but it does
require our cooperation and participation. Are we still going
to make mistakes? Sure we will. The purpose of this chapter

isn't to bring judgment on anyone. It's to challenge us to lift our sights higher. Instead of making excuses for our carnality and compromise, I want to offer a challenge to represent Jesus in this hour. This is the ultimate place of thinking big and acting big!

GO-BIG QUESTIONS

1. Jesus is looking for _____ on the face of our planet.

2. In order to accurately represent Christ through discipleship in people's lives there must be _____ in us.

3. Christ is transforming us from the inside out so that we can conform to His image of _____ in our generation.

4. How should you represent Jesus? Share your thoughts below.

_____

_____

_____

PART 3

GO BIG

THE MIND OF CHRIST FOR HOLY ACTION

A CALL TO HOLY ACTION

W E LOOKED AT the idea of thinking big in the first part of this book, and the next section talks about acting big. This brings us to the final section of this book on going big. When I think about this idea of *going*, I always think of missions.

Missions is all about going. Missions is all about holy action. Missions is a call from the heart of God. The more we embrace His heart, the clearer the call to holy action becomes.

In my life this has looked like an unquenchable passion to preach the gospel of Jesus Christ in the great nation of Russia. I just completed my one hundred and fifth trip to that great nation. I mentioned my first trip to Russia earlier in this book. It was during a time of monumental change. Unbelievably, the old Soviet system based on communism and repression was disintegrating rapidly. The nation was grappling with a new political and spiritual void.

For the first time in more than fifty years there was an opportunity for the gospel. The rigid resistance of atheism had dissolved. It was during this time that a call to holy action thundered from the throne of heaven. The body of Christ was being summoned to Russia. The unthinkable had happened: Russians could hear the gospel for the first time in my lifetime. The call to holy action required only one response—*go!* I can't say that I felt like the top candidate. Truthfully, my Russian is still quite limited; at the time it didn't exist. Many said it wasn't safe to travel during that tumultuous time. All I can say is that I said yes! And I have kept saying yes for the past twenty-five years.

I thank God for my dear friends Bob and Rob Hoskins with Book of Hope. They have both supernaturally been instruments in opening initial doors for me around the world. God loves Russia. I love Russia. It has been an honor and privilege to witness the move of God through the hearts of the Russian people. While there have been many great revivals, there are still so many that need to be reached with the love of God. This is true in every nation around the world. The call from heaven is still going out. Many more need to hear and respond to the gospel. The world needs Jesus desperately. Holy action is imperative.

Who will hear the call to holy action?

Who will respond?

Who will go?

We return to Romans 10. Thinking big and acting big is based on faith. These two variables give us the courage to go big. Paul states the open-ended promise "for whosoever shall call upon the name of the Lord shall be saved" (v. 13, KJV). The implications of this verse are massive. Salvation is open to all. No restrictions. No qualifications. Just simple faith reaching up to believe the Lord! The individual's decision determines everything. If anyone will call, God will save. This means there are only two options: either the person will call, or the person won't call. What will influence their decision? Faith in the Lord will determine everything.

Paul uses a very logical argument to develop this train of thought.

> How then shall they call on him in whom they have not believed? and how shall they believe in him of whom they have not heard? and how shall they hear without a preacher? And how shall they preach, except they be sent? As it is written, How beautiful are the feet of them that preach the gospel of peace, and bring glad tidings of good things!
>
> —ROMANS 10:14–15, KJV

The bottom line is going. *Salvation necessitates faith. Faith necessitates revelation. Revelation depends on communication.* Communication is the responsibility of a messenger. A messenger must be sent, but only if the messenger is willing to go! Heaven is ready to send; we must be willing to go.

A willingness to go is of great value to the Lord! Paul describes such an attitude when he quotes from Isaiah, saying,

"As it is written, 'How beautiful are the feet of those who preach the good news'" (Rom. 10:15). Feet that will go are beautiful to God! Feet that will share the message attract heaven's commendation! Feet that will communicate the good news are a prophetic fulfillment of Isaiah 52.

Going big for God is all about being a prophetic fulfillment of God's purposes to reach the nations! Heaven is still calling. Are we willing to let our feet move us to holy action?

Looking back I can see how God has used my life to make a big difference for His kingdom in Russia. Jesus has been glorified, lives have been changed, and a nation has been impacted in a big way. I responded to this call from heaven for holy action. Will you? Go big—believe.

GO-BIG QUESTIONS

1. Salvation necessitates _____.

2. Faith necessitates _____.

3. Revelation depends on _____.

4. How will you respond to your calling? Share your thoughts below.

_____

_____

_____

DAY 24
THE QUALIFICATION FOR HOLY ACTION

ONE OF THE biggest challenges concerning holy action is usually with ourselves. At some point during this process the idea of qualifications comes to the fore. We assume that going big must have some pretty big qualifications. Otherwise, why aren't more people doing it? And so our mind quickly generates a list of qualifications big enough to ensure that we aren't eligible for participation.

What are the qualifications for holy action? Who can actually go big for God in this generation? What kind of person can leave a legacy in this generation? These are all good questions.

Do we need a big bank account? Or the right educational background? Is our family upbringing important? Are there certain personality traits necessary?

The only qualification that Paul mentions in Romans 10 is that the messenger has to be willing to be sent (v. 15). Volition is always a question of the heart. In other words, willingness is a posture of the heart. As such, I believe that the real question concerning qualification is a heart issue.

The heart is vital in holy action. We have already explored several different heart postures in this book. Personally, I see the heart as the single greatest determining factor in living a big life. Thinking big is a condition of the heart. Acting big is also a condition of the heart. Likewise, going big is all about the heart! Specifically, I see three heart postures necessary for embracing holy action—bold, broken, and bright.

Let's look at the first component, boldness. *Being bold is essential for holy action.* Holy action is kingdom action, and kingdom action is not always easy. Peter had to stand up to a crowd comprising thousands of people and explain why his fellow disciples weren't drunk. A few days later he was imprisoned and beaten for preaching Jesus. Stephen confronted the religious of his day for their pride and narrow-mindedness. He was rewarded with stones and an instant promotion to glory. Jesus was hung on a tree as a criminal because of His commitment to the kingdom. What is the bottom line? Taking a stand for the King and His kingdom can be difficult! It requires courage. *Fear is one of the enemy's favorite tactics to destroy holy action.* It primarily affects the heart. The devil does everything he can to sideline our capacity for kingdom advancement through intimidation. The classic example is Timothy. The enemy used fear to paralyze this young man of holy action. Paul had to write a special letter to his spiritual son to remind him of the right posture of heart: boldness. He urged him to remember, "For God has not given us a spirit of fear, but of power and of love and of a sound mind" (2 Tim. 1:7, NKJV). *The key to experiencing a heart posture of boldness is consistent exposure to God's Spirit.* We need daily encounters with the Holy Spirit to shatter the spirit of fear.

The second posture is walking in brokenness, and it directly connects to the first, boldness. Courage is a direct result of being broken in God's presence. Take the example of King David. As he entered Jerusalem he was dancing in his undergarments before the ark, a symbol of God's manifest glory. His wife couldn't believe he was acting so undignified before the servants.

David's response is telling: "I will become even more undignified than this, and I will be humiliated in my own eyes" (2 Sam. 6:22, NIV). These are the words of a man comfortable with brokenness. His pride and sense of status had been shattered in the presence of God. He now had the courage to set his position aside and dance like mad for his God and King!

Sadly, for many believers the idea of brokenness disappears after their initial conversion and repentance. Many become consumed with external conformance to God's Word. It becomes nothing more than legalism and bondage when the Spirit isn't involved in the process. We separate ourselves from the world in our own strength. Slowly, pride creeps in because we feel that we have achieved sanctification in our own ability.

I contend that the single greatest excuse for escaping missions is so-called sanctification. The further the church gets away from the dirt of life, the farther we get away from a missional lifestyle. When I say "dirt" I mean the challenges, trials, sorrows, and suffering of our generation. I sometimes get myself into trouble when preaching by asserting that church has become a country club for people who can't afford one. The idea is that we withdraw from a hurting world.

The solution is brokenness. Brokenness keeps our boldness from becoming arrogance. Every new season of holy action in my life has always been preceded by a season of brokenness. Let me be clear what I mean by this. I'm not talking about egregious sin in my life. I would not be in the ministry if I had skeletons hidden in the closet of my heart. Nor am I talking about secret sin that I needed to repent of before the Lord. Sadly, brokenness has been exclusively associated with sin. Embracing holy action isn't about repenting of besetting sins, although that would certainly be a good starting point. Rather, it's about encountering the holiness of God in a fresh way. Brokenness is the result of my finite flesh experiencing His eternal holiness. Every time I encounter Him I become more aware of my desperate need of His grace.

I recently ministered in South Africa. God moved powerfully during some pastor's seminars and leadership conferences. The church buildings were packed with people experiencing a fresh touch from God. Yet, my most productive ministry during this period was with a group of homeless people. Other pastors accompanying me were astonished at the tangible connection taking place in the Spirit between this vagabond group of destitute people living on the streets and myself. What was the connection? Simply this: the guy speaking to them recognized that he was just as bad a sinner as they were. This is brokenness, an honest estimation of oneself in light of His majesty. This produces courage.

Finally, being bright is the result of walking in courage and brokenness. By being bright I mean that we reflect Jesus to a desperate world. Broken people experience His glory and make it known to those around them. They are able to magnify Jesus by reflecting the radiance of His presence. I'm fully convinced that what this world needs is not more highly qualified people.

Our world needs people with a broken, courageous heart to make His glory tangible. This is going big!

GO-BIG QUESTIONS

1. Being _____ is essential for holy action.

2. Fear is one of the _____ favorite tactics to destroy holy action.

3. The key to experiencing a heart posture of boldness is _____ being exposed to God's _____.

4. What does the Bible say about boldness? Share your thoughts below.

_____

_____

_____

DAY 25
PRAYER AND HOLY ACTION

RAYER IS VITAL *for holy action*. Without a posture of prayer holy action loses momentum. Prayer breathes a sacred element into our action. This divine component is what makes action more than just social work and nice activities. Prayer is the power source that makes our action holy. We must always be sure that our action is sanctioned by heaven and not just by humans.

Going big for God demands praying big with God. To be much with God enables us to do much for God and with God. Here is the critical component to prayer and critical action: partnership. Prayer responds to heaven's call to *go*. Holy action is heavenly sanctioned and earthly enacted. The two are unified in prayer.

Isaiah describes his personal encounter in prayer this way: "Then I heard the voice of the Lord saying, 'Whom shall I send? And who will go for us?' And I said, 'Here am I. Send me!'" (Isa. 6:8, NIV). The Lord revealed His glory to the prophet. Heaven was intersecting with Earth. Isaiah saw the Lord! He responded with brokenness and humility: "'Woe to me!' I cried. 'I am ruined! For I am a man of unclean lips, and I live among a people of unclean lips, and my eyes have seen the King, the LORD Almighty'" (v. 5, NIV).

Heaven responded with cleansing and calling. Notice the key word, *send*, in this passage. Heaven was looking for someone to commission on Earth. Isaiah responded immediately, "Here am I. Send me!" (v. 8, NIV). His willingness was met with the commission of holy action: "Go and tell this people" (v. 9, NIV).

Interestingly, Isaiah was already a prophet. This is not the diary of a pagan encountering God. He had already released some rather intensive prophecies concerning Judah and Israel. He had eschatological insight about the mount of the Lord in the Last Days. Chapter 1 indicates that he walked in great covenant revelation because he announced the forgiveness of sins. In other words, Isaiah had plenty of activity in his life. Most of it was good activity. Yet in a moment of brokenness, Isaiah moves in chapter 6 from good activity to a completely different level of sanctioned holy action. Prayer had placed heaven's priority before him. God was sending him to the nations!

Can you see the connection point in Isaiah's life between holy action and the nations? Prayer responds to God's glory and releases heaven's commission in our lives. This idea of prayer is important because prayer is all about partnership. It is the place for establishing the power of agreement. Heaven has a call. Heaven has a plan. Heaven is searching for someone to implement this plan and respond to this call.

The role of prayer is to bring us into agreement with the heart of God. Sadly, many believers have made prayer something completely different. Instead of agreeing with God's purpose, they are trying to force God to agree with their purpose. This borders on presumption and manipulation. Only arrogance or ignorance would attempt to dictate the purpose of God. Genuine prayer moves us and our purpose out of the way so that we can come into agreement with what heaven desires to accomplish.

As we touch the heart of God in the place of prayer we find heaven's priority again—intimacy. We are called first and foremost to know God and His character before we can make Him known. Once we have established this primary purpose, then God will release His commission for our lives. The holy action that comes from this posture of prayer is that He brings people into our lives that have also come into agreement with heaven. The end result is a three-way partnership: heaven, us, and the people God connects us with. These people help us walk in agreement with heaven's purposes.

I have seen this principle clearly in operation in my life. I have already mentioned the Book of Hope with the Hoskins family. In both cases, prayer had released a commission for holy action in the great nation of Russia. Since we were all in agreement with heaven's purpose to be accomplished there, it was easy for God to connect us together. In partnership we have seen God do some truly remarkable things to impact that land with the message of Christ. My ongoing relationship with them ensures that I continue to be properly aligned with what heaven is speaking and saying about Russia and the days ahead.

I also see this same dynamic of agreement in the place of confession. Jesus doesn't forgive our sins because our prayers are so sincere. Rather, the prayer of confession means that we bring our sins into agreement with what He says about them—namely, that our sins are in fact sin and that Jesus has already paid for them as we look to Him in confident trust for forgiveness. Once we get to this point, He can reveal His heart to us.

Holy action is all about the heart of God! Once we enter that glorious dimension of sharing His heart concerning our shared commission, ministry becomes much easier. It's no longer that I'm trying to impress people or put on a good performance. Rather, my going on His behalf becomes an opportunity to share His thoughts.

I was ministering at a church in the United States. At the close of the service many pressed in at the altar seeking God. The pastor had dismissed the worship team, thinking that my dear friend and traveling worship minister, James Huie, would be traveling with me. Unfortunately, he was not able to be there. Instead, a young lady who only knew four chords stood on the stage playing as we entered a time of ministry. She was doing her best, but it was quite a struggle.

I felt led to pray over different people. As I did I could sense God's heart. Different thoughts came to mind, and I prayed them over the people standing there. God's power descended as I prayed. These individuals were touched dramatically. The pastor came to me afterward astonished. He told me that he couldn't have better crafted a prayer to fit their situation than the one I prayed. He wanted to know how I did it considering the musical challenge.

My answer was simple: I came into agreement with the heart of God. Holy action must always be an overflow of the heart of God. Only then can we go big for God!

GO-BIG QUESTIONS

1. Prayer is vital for _____.

2. _____ big for God demands praying big with God.

3. The role of prayer is to bring us into _____ with the heart of God.

4. How can you make your prayer life more intimate? Share your thoughts below.

_____

_____

_____

VISION FOR HOLY ACTION

VISION IS ESSENTIAL when it comes to holy action. I like to define vision as "the capacity to see what heaven sees." It is the ability to see heaven's preferred future. God has a vision for our lives. This connects with the idea of prayer. Prayer gives us the perspective of heaven's vision. Heaven has a vision for our lives, our families, our churches, our cities, and our nations. Prayer lets us see what God sees. This is vitally important to keep our spirit alive.

Vision is the realm where hope comes alive. It is here that we see God's perspective. When we lose sight of heaven's perspective we quickly slide into one of two pitfalls: apathy or despondency. Apathy is the place of purposelessness because we are living visionless. Despondency is even worse. Not only are we living visionless but hopeless as well. The author of the Book of Proverbs makes this clear: "Without vision the people perish" (Prov. 29:18, author's paraphrase). This verse says that vision is the difference between life and death!

I like to talk about vision by asking three questions. All three are connected to the idea of holy action. The first question is this: How far can you see? This is an obvious vision question connecting sight to perception. It is the capacity to think thoughts far bigger than our current reality. It is dreaming dreams bigger than ourselves. The farther we see the farther we can go.

The second question is, How deep can you feel? This question is connected to compassion. It involves vision moving from the mental realm of the intellect and reaching the emotional aspect of the heart. It means vision touching the emotions. These two components together are explosive. It's like combining nitrogen and glycerin. The end result is dynamite of the heart in the form of holy action.

The third question touches on our emphasis in this section—action. How far are you willing to go? This deals with commitment and tenacity in implementing the vision that is exploding inside our heart. It enables us to go and go big! Challenges, obstacles, and setbacks are all overcome because we are going the full distance.

I often illustrate these questions by using the three parables that Jesus tells in Luke 15. The first parable is that of the lost sheep. The second one is related to a lost coin. And the third is the familiar story of a prodigal son. All three stories relate to the three questions we have identified.

The question, How far can you see? parallels the parable of the lost sheep. The shepherd recognized that only ninety-nine of his one hundred sheep were present and accounted for. In mathematical terms 99 percent is really good! The temptation was there for him to say, "It's just one sheep." No big deal, right? I think Jesus told this story to illustrate that the number one is of enormous value in heaven's economy. Vision must be able to see far enough to discern what heaven values as important. Without this critical component vision can become self-focused instead of God-focused.

The question, How deep can you feel? relates to the parable of a lost coin. I don't think that this was just any coin. My thought is that this coin had great emotional significance. Could it have been attached to a piece of jewelry that her husband had given her? Or maybe it was a part of her dowry? Or could it have been the family savings? In any case, her urgency to find the missing coin is only overshadowed by her joy in finding it. The value of this coin wasn't so much its financial significance as much as its relational significance. The coin represented so much more emotionally. She felt the loss of this coin in her heart, not just her pocket. Vision tugs on our heart strings through compassion.

The question, How far are you willing to go? is the question connected to the parable of the prodigal son. It is a picture of the relentless love of our Father to do whatever it takes. When the prodigal returned to confess his reckless lifestyle and sin, the father responded in remarkable fashion. The son expected servitude; the father offered him sonship. The servants were ordered to bring the best robe, a ring, and sandals for the reprobate. A celebration feast was planned in quick succession.

No expense was spared in demonstrating the father's tenacity and determination to have his son back again! Listen to the father's rationale for this lavish grace: "'For this son of mine was dead and is alive again; he was lost and is found'" (Luke 15:24, NIV).

Not only was the father willing to give of himself financially, but he was willing to surrender his reputation. The narrative tells us that while the son was still far away the Father ran toward him. Scholars tell us that it was unthinkable for a Jewish man to pull up his robe and run. Only in the direst of circumstances would this even be considered. Yet, the father withheld nothing, including his reputation, in order to ensure his son was restored. His affection in the form of an embrace, complete with a kiss, is the ultimate message of acceptance. No respectable Jew would behave this way, but it just didn't matter to the father.

Finally, the father jeopardized his relationship with his older son, knowing full well the way his reaction would be interpreted. Yet, his concern wasn't perception or the status quo; his concern was holy action! How far was he willing to go? The father was willing to do whatever it took for the prodigal to understand the message of sonship.

Luke 15 is powerful for one important reason. It contains moving illustrations of the lost being found. Holy action at its core is all about this singular pursuit—the lost must be found. All of our activity, programs, projects, and goals must have this one, singular ambition. We want to see the lost encounter the Father! This happens as we implement vision, compassion, and holy action.

Let me conclude this chapter by asking the questions again:

- How far can you see?

- How deeply can you feel?

- How far are you willing to go?

Go big—believe. It's an hour for holy action and vision.

GO-BIG QUESTIONS

1. How far you can see parallels the parable of
   the _____.

2. How deeply you can feel relates to the parable of
   a _____.

3. How far you are willing to go is the question connected to
   the _____.

4. What changes can you make in your life now to initiate
   holy action? Share your thoughts below.

_____

_____

_____

RISK AND HOLY ACTION

HOLY ACTION NEEDS another critically important variable: risk. Without it we may have holy vision and even holy compassion, but we will be dreamers without any holy action. Risk is the implementation stage that makes holy action more than a nice conversation piece. Risk demands our participation. It costs us the critic's seat by moving us center stage. Spectators are placed on the playing field.

Action must be authorized by heaven to make it holy risk. Our risk must be endorsed. Risk that is not based on God's Word is nothing more than spiritual gambling. We are, after all, talking about *holy* risk. This is connected to three words: *hearing, trusting,* and *obeying.* These three verbs move risk from something to be avoided to something to be pursued and acted on.

Holy risk starts with hearing the voice of God. Abram heard God telling him to leave Ur of the Chaldees and go into the unknown. Saul of Tarsus heard a similar voice on the road to Damascus. Each of us has also heard the voice of the Lord one way or the other. This connects to the idea of calling. The basic question behind all holy risk is this: Will I trust the Word of God?

Beyond this, hearing is being able to discern if we heard His voice accurately for our situation. This is a process developed in ongoing relationship with the Holy Spirit. This touches on the idea of prayer again. As we are properly aligned with heaven, we will hear the voice of the Spirit clearly.

Hearing is a very important step, but we have to move beyond it to the place of trust. This is where we have to grapple with the question found in every age: Can God be trusted? This is much deeper than just a simple mental assent. Trusting God involves His ultimate purposes for our lives—especially when they are different than what we expected.

The story of Abram is the classic example. In life's uncertainty and unpredictability, would he trust God? Would he trust God and leave his family to set out for the unknown? We have stories in Genesis of when he got it right, like on Mount Moriah with Isaac. In other places he got it miserably wrong, such as the story of his deception in Egypt. The lesson is that trust must be developed based on revelation of God's character. The more we grasp His nature the more we realize His intentions toward us are good. This produces the capacity for trust.

As the revelation of His character is established in our heart and mind, it becomes possible to hear His voice speaking things that require us to go outside of our comfort zone. Trust allows us see ourselves (vision) accomplishing the things we are hearing. This is not easy, but it is possible as we seek His heart. Risk on a heart level is being able to see the unseen. *As we get God's heart we can begin to see that which can't be seen naturally.* In other words, intimacy with God produces trust. We know Him. We love Him. We trust Him.

The third word is that of obedience. This is the critical moment when our trust is tested. Did we hear God accurately? Can His character be trusted in our situation? These two questions determine whether our faith will have the strength to stand and act. Holy action is obedience, the critical action step of response to what heaven has spoken. This is often the place of greatest testing.

Risk requires great tenacity. Often our situation will contradict our step of faith. This is where we take a step forward despite our circumstances. Risk is not easy. Paul puts it this way: "For we walk by faith, not by sight" (2 Cor. 5:7). Everyone loves to talk about faith until they reach the critical point of action. Often the pressures of what we see are just too much to warrant the risk. This is where we need the divine vision deposited in our heart to sustain us. Prayer also gives us the perseverance we need to press on despite the obstacles.

Some might ask if it is worth it. If risk can be so difficult, why actually bother implementing it? Wouldn't it be much safer just to sit back and watch? The answer to this question is found in the person of Christ. Jesus is all about holy action!

To play it safe and live a life of comfort circumvents the Cross. Can you imagine if Jesus had minimized the personal risk of the Cross? Too costly. Too painful. Too embarrassing. Too humiliating. There were many good reasons for not risking everything. Yet, in so doing, redemption would have been lost! This points to the other side of the risk, the reward of obedience. The cost of the risk determines the size of the reward. In Christ's life we see this principle in the prophecy found in Isaiah 53:11–12 about the suffering servant. Following the suffering of the Lamb of God, a promise is released:

> After he has suffered, he will see the light of life and be satisfied; by his knowledge my righteous servant will justify many, and he will bear their iniquities. Therefore I will give him a portion among the great, and he will divide the spoils with the strong, because he poured out his life unto death, and was numbered with the transgressors. For he bore the sin of many, and made intercession for the transgressors. (NIV)

Jesus's suffering on the cross has been rewarded with seeing many justified by His sacrifice. He now has a portion among the great. What is this portion? I believe it's the nations. People groups and tribes and tongues will be His spoils. The size of Christ's reward is enormous because of the price of the risk—His life.

Jesus calls us to be like Him. He calls us to holy action. Risk will always be involved in the equation. This chapter is an appeal not to run from it; rather, we are called to embrace it! When we place these three ideas together—hearing, trusting, and obeying—we see risk sparking holy action. Holy action leads to a glorious reward!

Abram was rewarded for walking by faith! God changed his name to Abraham, making him the father of faith as well as the father of nations!

Paul was rewarded for his obedience in the face of risk by seeing new congregations planted, people saved and established in the truth, and ultimately, God using his letters to inspire every believer in every generation and in every nation.

Risk is essential to holy action! Is it worth it? I certainly believe so.

Go big—believe.

GO-BIG QUESTIONS

1. Holy risk starts with hearing the _____ of God.

2. As we get God's heart we can begin to see that which can't be seen _____.

3. _____ requires great tenacity

4. Do you trust God enough to obey Him? Share your thoughts below.

_____

_____

_____

COMPASSION AND HOLY ACTION

COMPASSION IS DIRECTLY connected to holy action. We already discussed the role it plays a few chapters ago by asking the question, How deep can you feel? It plays a vital role in the implementation of vision. Having said this, it is also connected to God's love.

Compassion is the overflow of God's love igniting our hearts to action. Without God's love we won't have holy action. There may be action, but it will lack the holy. I like to say it this way: compassion is God's passionate love in action.

Paul described the necessity of love in 1 Corinthians 13, known as the love chapter. Paul was writing to spiritually minded believers in the church of Corinth. They prided themselves on having lots of spiritual activity in their meetings. Clearly, God's Spirit was at work among them, but due to compromise and strife, the work was corrupted. Paul offered a far better way, the way of love. He jumped right into the heart of the matter in verses 1–3:

> If I speak in the tongues of men or of angels, but do not have love, I am only a resounding gong or a clanging cymbal. If I have the gift of prophecy and can fathom all mysteries and all knowledge, and if I have a faith that can move mountains, but do not have love, I am nothing. If I give all I possess to the poor and give over my body to hardship that I may boast, but do not have love, I gain nothing. (NIV)

Notice Paul's argument here: spiritual power in the form of holy action must always be grounded by genuine love. Heavenly tongues are wonderful, as are linguistic skills for communication. Prophecy and discernment are necessary for edification. And thank God for faith that really can move mountains! This list sounds like holy action to me. What ministry wouldn't want to see all of these in operation? We would say, "Wow! What an anointing! What power! What glory in our midst! What a man or woman of God!"

Paul doesn't negate any of these gifts. Actually, he is validating their use for the people of God. Paul's contention is that all of the supernatural activity in the world lacks meaning if it isn't flowing from a place of love. In fact, he goes on to say that action for action's sake, even good action in the name of God, is worthless apart from love! It's nothing more than a resounding gong and a clanging cymbal—lots of noise and hype with no eternal gain for Christ or His kingdom.

This is a very difficult lesson for us to learn. We love the show. We enjoy the performance. The fireworks of ministry will bring a crowd, as well as the finances of the crowd. Yet, the seasoned missionary of the New Testament is reminding us that the deepest level of ministry is always connected to our question: How deep can you feel? The depths of our heart were created to feel, and feel deeply.

The deepest level is not satisfied by reputation or by physical satisfaction. We live in a generation in which many hearts want fame. This is a generation that wants to be known! This is an age that wants reputation and status. To be considered powerful and competent is prized. Likewise, many others seek sexual intimacy. This is a sex-crazed generation pursuing intimacy at all possible costs. We want to feel connected through physical pleasure.

The compassion of God is much deeper than either fame or physical satisfaction can provide in our life. Let me be clear in stating that God wants us fulfilled socially and physically, but our heart was designed for so much more. The deepest level of our heart can only be satisfied by compassion. Our heart will only be satisfied as it becomes a channel to release God's love.

Reputation and physical satisfaction will never do that. They will leave a vacuum in the heart that causes us to chase the wind. Compassion, however, will satisfy. The reason is because love transcends our selfishness. We are no longer seeking our own benefit but that of others. Compassion takes us outside of ourselves and forces us to grapple with God's glory and the needs of others to experience this glory.

Compassion will produce holy action in even the most difficult and hopeless of situations. This is because compassion is so much more than just feelings of sympathy. Jesus is our example. He was not just sad about certain situations, lamenting the despair of His generation. Rather, He ministered from a place of compassion; this produced holy action. His heart was moved, and action was released.

We see this principle in action in Matthew 14:14: "When Jesus landed and saw a large crowd, he had compassion on them and healed their sick" (NIV). Notice the sequence of Matthew's description. Christ felt deeply; holy action exploded.

A few chapters later in Matthew 20 we see Jesus leaving Jericho. Two blind men made a scene, calling out to Him unreservedly. Jesus asked what they wanted, and of course, they want to see again. Before the healing in this story that we know and love is a key moment. Verse 34 tells us that Jesus had compassion on them. His heart was moved. The next thing He did was touch their eyes. This is holy action.

Again, in Mark 8:2-3 we see this parallel between compassion and holy action: "I feel compassion for the people because they have remained with Me now three days and have nothing to eat" (NASU). His compassion led to four thousand people receiving a supernatural meal.

We see Him standing outside of Lazarus's tomb. One of His best friends was dead. What follows next is the shortest verse in the Bible, describing Jesus's compassion: "Jesus wept" (John 11:35). Yet, these were no ordinary tears of despair and hopelessness. These were tears of compassion. In short succession the dead man would be walking again. Jesus cried into the portal of death, the tomb, and ordered Lazarus's soul to return into his lifeless body. Verse 44 tells us that the dead man came out!

The bottom line is this: pay attention to what God puts in your heart. Your compassion will produce His holy action through you! Lives will be changed. People will encounter Jesus.

Go big—believe!

GO-BIG QUESTIONS

1. Compassion is the _____ of God's love igniting
    our hearts to action.

2. The deepest level of _____ is not satisfied by
    reputation or by physical _____.

3. Compassion produces holy action in even the most
    _____ and _____ of situations.

4. When is the last time you showed compassion to another?
    Share your thoughts below.

    _____

    _____

    _____

HOLY ACTION AND THE MIRACULOUS

I N TALKING ABOUT compassion and holy action in the previous chapter we have identified one of the key marks of holy action: the miraculous. When I talk about the miraculous I mean God's supernatural intervention. Compassion sets the stage for God to show up and show off as only He can do!

His power being demonstrated is critical in this hour. The body of Christ has much fine-sounding teaching and lots of energetic preaching. We have large facilities and lots of activities. What seems to be much more difficult to come by in this critical moment of human history is the miraculous. We need demonstrations of God's power and authority that will confirm the truth of His Word!

Listen to Paul's take on this idea in 1 Corinthians 2:1–5:

> And so it was with me, brothers and sisters. When I came to you, I did not come with eloquence or human wisdom as I proclaimed to you the testimony about God. For I resolved to know nothing while I was with you except Jesus Christ and him crucified. I came to you in weakness with great fear and trembling. My message and my preaching were not with wise and persuasive words, but with a demonstration of the Spirit's power, so that your faith might not rest on human wisdom, but on God's power. (NIV)

What would our defense of our ministry or church look like in the twenty-first century? Would we claim that we are valid ministers of the gospel because we are family friendly? Or would we say that we have dynamic preaching and teaching gifts? Or possibly that we have lots of financial resources? Or maybe that we have media coverage and name recognition? Of course, none of these things are bad. My point is that

Paul's defense of his ministry was based on demonstration not reputation.

Demonstration marked his ministry as an apostle of Christ. In 2 Corinthians he tells the church that he is a genuine apostle. Apparently, the church was full of charlatans and big talkers. They were trying to destroy Paul's influence in Corinth. Paul's response follows the demonstration argument again. He said, "I persevered in demonstrating among you the marks of a true apostle, including signs, wonders and miracles" (2 Cor. 12:12, NIV).

Let's be clear. *There is much more to an apostle than just signs and wonders.* Character and integrity matter greatly. Intimacy with Christ is paramount. Yet, let's not overlook the fact that Paul lists the miraculous as one of the primary qualifications of the apostolic.

Why is any of this important? I believe that holy action in Christ's name must also be marked by the miraculous.

Jesus instructed His disciples to go and preach the gospel to all nations. It is what we commonly refer to as the Great Commission. It is a partnership idea. *Commission* implies a combined mission between Earth and heaven. Missions is all about partnership between us and Him. Most believers are comfortable with the idea of missions and even believe that it is an important aspect of following Christ. Yet, there is more to Christ's commission than just nice teaching and preaching and serving globally. There is even more to it than an evangelistic emphasis, as important as that is.

In Mark 16 Jesus attaches a demonstration component as well.

> And these signs will accompany those who believe: in my name they will cast out demons; they will speak in new tongues; they will pick up serpents with their hands; and if they drink any deadly poison, it will not hurt them; they will lay their hands on the sick, and they will recover.
>
> —MARK 16:17–18

We are called to partner with Him in the supernatural demonstration of the gospel as well.

The Book of Hebrews instructs us to fix our thoughts on Jesus. Hebrews 3:1 gives us the full thought: "Therefore, holy brothers and sisters, who share in the heavenly calling, fix your thoughts on Jesus, whom we acknowledge as our apostle and high priest" (NIV).

Jesus is our Apostle and High Priest. We are called to be like Him. This involves the mind and the heart. We have talked much about this. In this process of becoming like Christ we are becoming an apostolic people. As already mentioned, there is much more to the apostolic than just the miraculous. Yet, without demonstration one must ask the question of whether or not we are truly manifesting Christ's presence and accomplishing His missional mandate.

Something is wrong in the house of the Lord if miracles are the exception. Demonstration is just as necessary now as it would have been some twenty centuries ago. *The Word of God hasn't changed.* The power of God isn't restricted because of the digital age. Jesus's nature certainly hasn't morphed.

So why does demonstration seem so limited in many places? I believe that the simplest answer is that we aren't thinking Christ's thoughts and sharing His heart. We must cultivate this dynamic in the place of prayer. There is a direct correlation between intimacy and demonstration. Holy action explodes when we align ourselves with His heart and think His thoughts! This is an hour for demonstration.

Go big—believe!

GO-BIG QUESTIONS

1. There is much more to an _____ than just signs and _____.

2. The Book of Hebrews instructs us to fix our thoughts on _____.

3. The Word of God hasn't _____.

4. Why is it so important to think Christ's thoughts? Share your thoughts below.

_____

_____

_____

DAY 30
HOLY ACTION AND THE HARVEST

JOHN 4 PAINTS a very interesting picture for us. Jesus was standing by a well in the heat of the day engaging in a conversation with a woman attempting to draw water from the well. She was a Samaritan. Jesus was in Samaria among a people group that were considered half-castes by His peers. They were unreachable and untouchable to the entire Jewish nation.

The disciples were shocked to see Jesus talking. Even the average Jew viewed the Samaritans as not worthy of a greeting, let alone a conversation. In their minds the only thing more unthinkable than talking with a Samaritan was the fact that Jesus was talking with a Samaritan woman. Nothing about the context of this story would make any sense to any reasonable Jew. A rabbi talking with a Samaritan woman of questionable character? Just what was Jesus thinking?

Clearly, Jesus saw things very differently. The subject of His conversation with the disciples is of great interest for us. What would Jesus talk about after His interaction with this woman? Would it be His need for some lunch? Or possibly instructions for not being left alone in the future? Criticism of this woman's shameful past? No. Only one thing figured in His mind at that moment: harvest. Jesus wanted the disciples to understand that they were not ready for the response of the city. The disciples were ready for Jesus. The city was ready for Jesus. But the disciples were not ready for the city.

> Don't you have a saying, "It's still four months until harvest"? I tell you, open your eyes and look at the fields! They are ripe for harvest. Even now the one who reaps draws a wage and harvests a crop for eternal life, so that the sower and the reaper may be glad together.
>
> —JOHN 4:35–36, NIV

Jesus mentions the word *harvest* directly some three times in two verses. He mentions it indirectly through the words *reap, sower, reaper,* and *field* as allusions of harvest another several times. The lesson seems clear: Where others see stigma, Jesus sees harvest. When others see *inaccessible,* Jesus sees harvest. His priority is always harvest!

In this story the harvest is possible despite cultural stereotypes by one sure means: holy action! At the beginning of John 4 it is holy action on the part of Christ. By the end of John 4 it is a commission communicated to the disciples. No longer can prejudices and stereotypes be grounds for avoiding holy action. In the kingdom the harvest trumps all such personal or cultural notions.

This is a critical point that we must get our mind around. *When Jesus looks at our world and the situations of our world He's not thinking politically or socioeconomically. He's thinking about harvest.* This is His heartbeat; this is His eternal priority. Harvest is the overflow of the kingdom. When the King and His kingdom take possession of our life there is only one possible outcome: participation in the harvest fields of our world. We have many good focuses in the body of Christ today: health and wellness, discipleship, pastoral training, leadership development, kid's ministry, youth ministry, college ministry, men's ministry, women's ministry, feeding projects, orphanages, foster care, prayer, cultural engagement, and missions, just to name a few. All of these must never lose sight of the one overarching goal of Christ's heart, harvest.

This whole book is built on the simple thought that we as believers are called to share Christ's heart and thoughts. As we learn to share His heart and think His thoughts, I can guarantee you that sooner or later harvest will come to the fore. Jesus is passionate about it. We must be too.

This is a season unlike any other in our world. The challenges and struggle of this hour are clearly portrayed everywhere. Economic recession, terrorism, racism, war, rebellion, perversion, and tyranny have become part of everyday life in many places. Fear and intimidation seek to strangle this generation. As followers of Christ we must maintain His perspective. This is the greatest hour of evil the world has ever known, but it will also be the greatest hour of harvest the world has ever known. Heaven will use all of these events for one sure purpose: many will enter the kingdom of God.

If we are going to think Christ's thoughts and share His heart, then we will become like Him. If we become like Him then we will make ourselves available to participate in the harvest. This is where we connect with His great commission. *Heaven is all about harvest*; therefore, heaven must have our participation.

I watched God unfold this lesson many years ago in the city of Luhansk, Ukraine. Our eyes burned with fatigue after many hours of flying. Despite our physical exhaustion, our spirits were invigorated as we landed in Kiev, Ukraine. Laughter and anticipation filled the conversation of the Book of Hope team. We were on our way to Luhansk, Ukraine, for a Book of Hope Celebration in the city auditorium. Each day we would visit all the schools in the city with the precious gift of the Book of Hope for every child, teenager, college student, and their teachers, inviting them to the celebration at night and, most importantly, planting a new church.

I had sent television programs and radio advertisements announcing the celebration months in advance of this trip. We had sent tens of thousands of Books of Hope ahead of us.

When we arrived in Luhansk, all the hard work seemed to evaporate due to the news we received. The school systems had been closed to us, the city had refused to allow the TV programs to run, and the airlines had lost our luggage. There would be no way to distribute the materials.

Our team decided to pray in shifts all night. I could hear people walking the hallways all night praying for God to intervene. Early the next morning our team joined in corporate prayer before breakfast. We walked around the corner to the restaurant that had been contracted to feed us, only to find it closed. Not only were our hearts disappointed, but now we also had empty stomachs.

Eugene, our interpreter, found a restaurant that agreed to make us some boiled eggs with brown bread and hot tea. It was a small step of encouragement. Back at the hotel we continued in prayer, asking God to open a door.

After another hour one of the interpreters came in. She had been talking on the phone to different schools about us coming to give them the Book of Hope. "Let's go! There's a school expecting us now!" Irene announced.

We were surprised to find many people standing in the front of the school to greet us after so many challenges and disappointments. Everyone seemed happy about our arrival, and a television crew was also there to interview me. The principal of the school told us that this was the best school in the city and wanted us to come there first.

Before entering the school the teachers brought a fresh baked round loaf of hot bread, which is a Ukrainian custom to welcome special guests. I broke a piece off and dipped it in salt, saying, "It is great to be in the great city of Luhansk! Thank you for inviting us." The teachers clapped as the TV crew filmed. We entered the school and sat down for an interview with the local reporter.

The interview went well, and at the end the journalist interviewing me turned to the camera and announced in Russian, "The television station would sponsor the Book of Hope evening Celebration in the city auditorium. Everyone needs to attend." God had heard our prayers!

The principal entered the room immediately afterward to let us know it was time for the assembly. When we walked into the auditorium there were hundreds in attendance, filling every seat and overflowing to standing-room-only capacity.

I spoke of the love and power of Jesus and how He could cleanse our sins if we surrender our lives to Him. After I finished I gave an invitation to everyone to come that night to the Book of Hope Celebration.

The principal walked over to me in front of the entire school and asked, "How do you become a Christian?" I smiled and replied, "You pray by inviting Jesus into your heart and ask Him to forgive you of your sins." The principal continued, "Do you know this prayer, and can you teach us?"

All communication occurring was happening with an interpreter in front of the crowd.

I answered, "We must give everyone an opportunity to surrender their life to Jesus." Without hesitation the principal turned to the school and asked everyone who wanted to become a Christian to lift their hand. Hands shot up everywhere! As we prayed I was overwhelmed at the goodness of God, sensing the best was yet to come.

After we returned to the school office, one of the staff members asked if he could tell me his story: "Two years ago on vacation I was on a train and met a man visiting our country who was a Christian. We talked about God for two hours on the train. When he asked me about accepting Jesus into my own heart I refused. As I left that day something inside me changed, and I prayed this prayer: 'God if you are real, send someone to my city and to my school to teach us the truth.' Today you are the answer to my prayer."

There is a man somewhere in the world that planted the seed in that man's heart for Jesus. He participated in the purpose of the kingdom. His efforts opened every school in Luhansk. During the evening celebrations 7,432 people surrendered their lives and invited Jesus into their hearts! This is holy action that produced a glorious harvest.

GO-BIG QUESTIONS

1. When Jesus looks at our _____ and the situations of our world He's thinking _____.

2. If we are going to think Christ's _____ and share His heart, then we will become like _____.

3. Heaven is all about _____.

4. How does making Christ's priorities your priorities change your perspective on life? Share your thoughts below.

_____

_____

_____

EPILOGUE

THERE IS NO greater subject than Jesus. He is our example. His life is our inspiration. His commission is our obsession. There has never been a more perfect model of faith. As we embrace His perfect sacrifice in confident trust, we experience the new life of Christ.

This new life transforms us from the inside out, empowering us to be like Jesus in this generation. It is a holy calling. His life flows through us into those around us, providing them the same opportunity for transformation.

I want to see a move of God in this generation. What will it take? How will we see darkness being pushed back by light? When will lost people be found? What will signal slaves of sin being set free? When will the harvest overtake the reaper? I believe with all my heart that it involves God's people embracing God's heart and putting it into action in this generation.

This book is an appeal to believers of all ages, backgrounds, and traditions to move beyond a place of admiration and into a place of manifestation. We are called to represent Jesus! We are called to think His thoughts, implement His actions, and follow His direction. As we do this we are going to see the heavens open to touch the Earth, producing a glorious harvest.

This is an hour for *big faith* that will be answered by a *big God!* So what are we waiting for? Think big—believe! Act big—believe! Go big—believe!

GO-BIG ANSWERS

INTRODUCTION
THE POWER OF THOUGHTS

1. seed
2. kingdom greatness
3. perpetual destruction
4. grace of God

DAY 1
THE HEART

1. we were given His righteousness to reign and abide in our lives
2. Mercy
3. able / Jesus took our sins and died for us on the cross

DAY 2
GOD'S PROMISE FOR THE NEW HEART

1. The heart / generated
2. condition of the heart
3. the ability to experience a new heart

DAY 3
THE TRANSFORMATION OF THE HEART

1. transformed heart
2. voluntary state of mind
3. fearful / insecure

DAY 4
THE POWER OF FAITH

1. power of God / believes
2. anyone
3. faith

DAY 5
TO BELIEVE OR NOT TO BELIEVE

1. Faith, obedience
2. faith to move us far beyond a place of mental acceptance
3. believe / the faithfulness of God and His Word

DAY 6
BELIEF AND THE FOUNDATION OF COVENANT

1. substance
2. know
3. believe / lordship

DAY 7
BELIEF AND THE EXPERIENCE OF GLORY
1. Being born again
2. unimportant
3. the kingdom of God

DAY 8
BELIEF AND SURRENDER
1. empty formality / rigid religiosity
2. sinful / replaces / heart
3. wholly / solely / reservation

DAY 9
BELIEF AND DIRECTION
1. banks
2. receiving
3. Word / direction

DAY 10
BELIEF AND A WORD-FILLED HEART
1. big / make
2. victory / Satan
3. Word / power

DAY 11
BELIEF AND AN OVERFLOWING HEART
1. giving / receiving
2. kingdom
3. His supply of grace

DAY 12
BELIEF AND THE ACTION OF FAITH
1. faith / action
2. right
3. authentic action

DAY 13
MOMENTUM: THE ACTION OF FAITH
1. moving object
2. obedience / avalanche
3. more

DAY 14
THE SEED OF THE WOMAN: TRANSFORMATION FOR OUR FEET
1. our victory
2. good news / warfare
3. crush Satan

Day 15
The Seed of Abraham: Transformation for Our Hands
1. devil / God / humanity
2. curse / hands
3. weapons

Day 16
The Seed of David: Transformation for Our Heart
1. leader / worshiper / champion
2. God's kingdom
3. heart of intimacy

Day 17
Transformation in Vertical Relationship
1. history / testimony
2. present
3. prayer life

Day 18
Transformation in Horizontal Relationships
1. expression / relationships
2. surrender / glory
3. heart / us

Day 19
Transformation in Internal Relationship
1. God / ourselves
2. peace / oneself
3. Fragmentation / multiple

Day 20
Transformation in Thinking
1. think / thinks
2. humility
3. attitude

Day 21
Transformation of Love
1. wounded / hurt
2. transforms
3. thoughts

Day 22
The Challenge of Transformation
1. representation
2. transformation
3. holiness

DAY 23
A CALL TO HOLY ACTION
1. faith
2. revelation
3. communication

DAY 24
THE QUALIFICATION FOR HOLY ACTION
1. bold
2. enemy's
3. consistently / Spirit

DAY 25
PRAYER AND HOLY ACTION
1. holy action
2. Going
3. agreement

DAY 26
VISION FOR HOLY ACTION
1. lost sheep
2. lost coin
3. prodigal son

DAY 27
RISK AND HOLY ACTION
1. voice
2. naturally
3. Risk

DAY 28
COMPASSION AND HOLY ACTION
1. overflow
2. feeling / satisfaction
3. difficult / hopeless

DAY 29
HOLY ACTION AND THE MIRACULOUS
1. apostle / wonders
2. Jesus
3. changed

DAY 30
HOLY ACTION AND THE HARVEST
1. world / harvest
2. thoughts / Him
3. harvest

NOTES

ACKNOWLEDGMENTS

1. "The New Heart" may be found in *The World's Greatest Sermons, Vol. 5: Guthrie to Mozley*, Grenville Kleiser, ed. (New York: Funk & Wagnalls Co., 1908), 1–22.

INTRODUCTION
THE POWER OF THOUGHTS

1. Bruce Davis, "There Are 50,000 Thoughts Standing Between You and Your Partner Every Day!" *The Huffington Post*, May 23, 2013, http://www.huffingtonpost.com/bruce-davis-phd/healthy-relationships_b_3307916.html (accessed March 9, 2017).

DAY 2
GOD'S PROMISE FOR THE NEW HEART

1. *The World's Greatest Sermons, Vol. 5: Guthrie to Mozley*, s.v. "The New Heart."

DAY 5
GOD'S PROMISE FOR THE NEW HEART

1. "Hebrew Definitions," *Precept Austin*, s.v. "believe," http://www.preceptaustin.org/hebrew_definitions (accessed March 22, 2017).
2. Ibid.
3. Ibid.
4. Ibid.
5. Ibid.
6. Ibid.
7. Charles Spurgeon, "Sermon 766," *The Complete Works of C. H. Spurgeon, Vol. 13: Sermons 728 to 787* (Harrington, DE: Delmarva Publications, Inc., 2013).

DAY 6
BELIEF AND THE FOUNDATION OF COVENANT

1. "The KJV New Testament Greek Lexicon," *Bible Study Tools*, s.v. "homologeo," http://www.biblestudytools.com/lexicons/greek/kjv/homologeo.html (accessed March 22, 2017).
2. Chuck Swindoll and Roy B. Zuck, Eds., *Understanding Christian Theology* (Nashville, TN: Thomas Nelson, 2003).

DAY 8
BELIEF AND SURRENDER

1. "Lexicon: Strong's H3519 – Kabowd," *Blue Letter Bible*, https://www.blueletterbible.org/lang/lexicon/lexicon.

cfm?strongs=h3519 (accessed April 16, 2017).
2. Ibid.

DAY 13
MOMENTUM: THE ACTION OF FAITH

1. Oxford University Press, *Oxford Living Dictionaries: English*, s.v., "momentum," https://en.oxforddictionaries.com/definition/momentum (accessed March 22, 2017).

DAY 20
TRANSFORMATION IN THINKING

1. Chuck Swindoll, "Attitude," quoted in David Hoyt, "Attitude—It's a Choice!" *The John Maxwell Co.*, July 31, 2014, http://www.johnmaxwell.com/blog/attitude-its-a-choice (accessed March 22, 2017).
2. Oxford University Press, Oxford Living Dictionaries Online, s.v. "attitude," https://en.oxforddictionaries.com/definition/attitude (accessed March 22, 2017).

DAY 21
TRANSFORMATION OF LOVE

1. Raphael Ben Levi, *Romance of the Hebrew Calendar* (Bloomington, IN: XLibris, 2013) 263. For the spelling of the Hebrew phrase, see "I Am to My Beloved," *Jewish Treats*, National Jewish Outreach Program, September 15, 2011, http://www.jewishtreats.org/2011/09/i-am-to-my-beloved.html (accessed March 22, 2017).
2. Ibid., 264.
3. Ibid.

ABOUT THE AUTHOR

MIKEL IS A part of the global outpouring of God. His ministry has sparked movements of spiritual awakening all across America and around the world. He has conducted crusades in France, Sweden, Russia, Romania, Poland, Ukraine, Moldova, Serbia, Germany, South Africa, Malawi, the Philippines, Hong Kong, Taiwan, Haiti, Japan, Singapore, India, and Thailand and has been actively involved with OneHope's work in Russia for over two decades.

Mikel has a creative and unique fresh anointing coupled with a sound balance of humor, which ministers to adults and youth alike. God also uses Mikel in a powerful way of teaching and leading thousands of people each year in receiving the baptism of the Holy Spirit. He preaches with fire, passion, and an anointed gifting to draw the lost into the kingdom of God. He emphasizes evangelism and inspires revival that refuels, energizes, and generates an anticipation and atmosphere for God to move in the miraculous.

Mikel French Ministries has assisted in distributing The Book of Hope to 4 million students in Russia, where there is a great transformation in the next generation. Through the generous support of partners, he has presented the message of Jesus Christ to millions of people in the nation of Russia through televised citywide soul-winning celebrations.

Mikel French Ministries is also involved extensively in the ongoing vision of planting and establishing churches in Russia. Mikel considers it an honor to assist in conducting an annual pastors' conference, where thousands of pastors from Russia's eleven time zones come for training, teaching, and equipping.

Mikel and his wife, Marsha, reside in Tulsa, Oklahoma. They have one goal and one mission: world evangelism.

CONTACT THE AUTHOR

contactmikel@mikelfrench.org

(918) 355-6083

Twitter: @JMikelFrench

Facebook: Mikel French Ministries

Web: www.MikelFrench.org

Instagram: Mikel_French